WORD *of* MOUTH

Poems Featured on NPR's

All Things Considered

Edited and Introduced by

CATHERINE BOWMAN

Vintage Books

A Division of Random House, Inc.

New York

First Vintage Books Edition, March 2003

Copyright © 2003 by Catherine Bowman

All rights reserved under International and Pan-American
Copyright Conventions. Published in the United States by
Vintage Books, a division of Random House, Inc., New York,
and simultaneously in Canada by Random House
of Canada Limited, Toronto.

Vintage and colophon are registered trademarks of Random House, Inc.

National Public Radio, NPR, npr and All Things Considered are federally registered
service marks of National Public Radio, Inc., and may not be used without permission.

Library of Congress Cataloging-in-Publication Data
Word of mouth : poems featured on NPR's
All things considered / edited and introduced by
Catherine Bowman. — 1st Vintage Books ed.
p. cm.
ISBN 0-375-71315-8
1. American poetry—20th century. I. Bowman, Catherine.
II. All things considered (Radio program)
PS615 .W646 2003
811'.508—dc21
2002028077

Book design by JoAnne Metsch

www.vintagebooks.com

Printed in the United States of America
10 9 8 7 6 5 4

this poem waits for you to cross over
to cross over love, this poem waits for you
to cross over, to cross over love
this poem waits for you to crossover
too crossover, too, love

—Quincy Troupe

CONTENTS

hat is a poem? People often ask me that, and I always feel that it's one of those easy questions that's impossible to answer, like trying to define or dissect a kiss. Donald Hall calls a poem a deliciousness of the senses. Emily Dickinson wrote in a letter: "If I feel physically as if the top of my head were taken off, I know that is poetry." William Carlos Williams believed a poem was a little machine made out of words. Laura Howard, a young poet in one of my classes, called a poem a brand-new pair of red go-go boots. Here's Coleridge's famous definition of poetic imagination: "a repetition in the finite mind of the eternal act of creation in the infinite I Am." Robert Frost said poetry is a wild tune, a necessary stay against confusion. But definition and denotation are the enemies of poetry; one can only reach an approximation, for it's like trying to pin down what is constantly moving, shifting, vital, protean—

Over the years, introducing poets to a wide audience on National Public Radio (NPR), I discovered that what is most interesting about poetry right now in America is the remarkable polyphonic medley of voices and audiences. I wasn't interested in reporting or touting the pickings from particular literary trends, the academic marketplace, or certain aesthetic schools. To declare the three or four top voices that will live on didn't seem pertinent to the task at hand, nor did it accurately convey what is going on in the country. Instead, as a practitioner and lover of poetry, I wanted to offer a wide range of voices showing how varied the imagination can be, how complex and full of possibility. That is to say, the poems in this book are not composed around a commonly agreed middle C. Instead, these poems—sometimes tuneful, sometimes hymnal, other times raucous and scraping—harmonize on the racket and cacophony of our times in an admixture of seduction, heartbreak, consolation, and wisdom. In the marvelous way they attend to the world, these poems make a love-music that undermines generalizations and presuppositions about poetry and about the voices behind the poems. For example, the most passionate and profound love poems in the collection are by poets over the age of sixty.

If anything, considering the contents of this book, a poem could be defined as a conversation. Muriel Rukeyser called poetry "a meeting place." A meeting place where conversations can take place between the poem and the reader; between imaginations, identities, landscapes, borders, and boundaries; between the world of personal experience, such as dreams and private perceptions, and the world of data-based historically recorded fact; a conversation on life and its irrevocable choices. Rukeyser says, "A poem invites you to feel. More than that: it invites you to respond. And better than that: a poem invites total response. Poetry asks us to feel and it asks us to respond." This is a conversation full of wonder and nourishment, and you are invited to engage with the questions and answers grafted between the lines and images. Listening to or reading a poem is an invitation for both poem and reader to engage in what Octavio Paz calls "two moments of a single reality."

Often this conversation is uneasy, asks tough questions. Many of the writers included here have lived through hardships, abuse, poverty, illness, and the devastation of racism and war; yet in spite of their grappling with life's pain, we also hear the rocking solace of a lullaby: the poet transcending sorrow through the music of language—through song.

Former U.S. Poet Laureate Robert Pinsky has said, "Poetry is a vocal, which is to say a bodily art. The medium of poetry is a human body: the column of air inside the chest, shaped into signifying sounds in the larynx and the mouth. In this sense, poetry is just as physical or bodily an art as dancing." Listeners of NPR have told me over and over that hearing poems read out loud offered a way into poetry they had not discovered through simply reading; they discovered new ways to experience the poem. To take the poem off the page and into the airwaves gives us a way to participate in the physicality of the poem. There is, I believe, a return to poetry's earlier origins and roots in the spoken word, as it attempts to resist the mind/body split that typifies so much of our lives and public discourse.

The voice mediated through the telephone, the microphone, the radio, the tape recorder, the webstream, and other sound technologies; the modernists' and post–World War II poets' impulse to create a poetry based on the rhythms of American speech; and a desire to return to so-called primitive poetry of spoken ritual and spirituality: all these point to a growing emphasis on the oral nature of poetry. Eliot's "The Waste Land" was originally titled "He Do the Police in Different Voices." Langston Hughes created a literary verse form out of the blues. The spoken, oral aspects of poetry were essential to the work of such poets as Frank O'Hara, Denise Levertov, Ricardo Sanchez, Charles Olson, Amiri Baraka, and Alan Ginsberg with their emphasis on talking, breath, folk forms, organic physical structures, and musical vocalizations. Ginsberg and Robert Creeley said the inspiration for their poetic line came not from iambic pentameter but from listening to bebop. Jayne Cortez, Sonia Sanchez, and Quincy Troupe often collaborate and perform with musicians and composers. In this sense, NPR has done something quite radical and avant-garde by following the lead of the poets and allowing us to experience the poem off the page in a way that is both rhythm-based and meaning-based. For in poetry, rhythm is the highest form of meaning. In an essay called "Poetry & the Microphone," George Orwell says, "if true poetry could be introduced to the big public in such a way as to make it seem *normal* . . . then part of the prejudice against it might be overcome."

In the spring of 1995, NPR's *All Things Considered*® invited me to be their on-the-air "poet-reporter" for an ongoing series on contemporary poetry. This book is a collection of the poems and poets we have showcased since 1995. (Some of the poems that we recorded but could not air because of time restraints are also included here.) In these five- to ten-minute segments, broadcast to an audience of over eight million worldwide, NPR listeners would usually hear three or four poems recorded by the author in the studio. My job was to act as a kind of Poetry DJ, introducing the poems and poet, and then commenting in a chat-style format, usually with *All Things Considered* hosts Linda Wertheimer and Noah Adams. The poetry showcase not only quickly and inexpensively featured a whole array of poets, but also talked about poetry in a casual, nonacademic manner, offering people not only poems to listen to, but also a model in which to talk about poetry without being pretentious and rarified, keeping it conversational.

I first started thinking about this project when I was living on a ranch in the Texas Hill Country and working on a new book of poems. Most evenings, I would sit on the front porch meditating on the limestone and granite cliffs, mottled with live oak and the gnarly cedar. Colossal long-horn steer, souvenirs from the old west, would wander like clockwork through the yard from the next-door ranch. I listened to the radio a lot, and I started wondering why I never heard any poetry on the radio. Looking up at the big Texas sky, I remembered many years as a kid with the transistor radio up to my ear listening to late-night FM as I imagined the world and all of its animals asleep. This is the same feeling of reverie I have when reading poetry, a feeling of transcending time and space into various other worlds and frequencies. Most of all, poetry, with its great compression and linguistic music, seemed just right for the radio. Real poetry was being written and read more than ever before, but why the invisibility in the mainstream media? My suspicion was that it had more to do with marketing and exposure and the current critical discourse around poetry, than with poetry's decline as a cultural force in people's lives.

My home at the time was in New York City, where I had been working as a poet-in-the-schools with Teachers & Writers Collaborative. An itinerant poetry lady, I traveled all over New York City, from elementary schools in the South Bronx to the High School for Pregnant and Parenting Teens in East New York, and during these residencies I had observed the absolute pleasure and joy young people found in reading and writing poetry. I also loved going to poetry readings. There was an exciting scene burgeoning downtown. On any given Friday night, at the Nuyorican Poets Café, Miguel Algarín and Bob Holman would introduce the packed room to exciting new voices—bringing poetry off the page, onto the stage—challenging notions about where poetry comes from, who has access to it, who writes, it and who reads it. Uptown, there were the more established but equally exciting readings sponsored by the Academy of American Poets or the Ninety-second Street Y. These series, plus many others, both uptown and downtown, came out of the work of poets and arts activists like Paul Blackburn and Elizabeth Cray, who early on understood the significance of reading poetry out loud and recording it. Currently, on any given night there are poetry readings and open mics in cities all over the country. Perhaps this resurgence and interest in the spoken word is bigger than poetry. Maybe it has to do with a human need, a real hunger for a genuine physical experience of language itself.

When I returned to New York from Texas, my husband, Andy Biskin, helped me make a cassette tape of five poets reading their poems along with very brief recorded introductions. One of the poets was the late Joseph Brodsky, whom we recorded on my Walkman one afternoon at our dining room table over coffee. My idea was simply to showcase the poems, to hear the poet reading his or her work. When I sent the tape in to NPR I was acting as an advocate of poetry more than anything else. A few days later *All Things Considered* producer Margaret Low Smith called saying they liked my ideas but wanted one small change: they wanted me to introduce the poets and talk a little about the poems. It turned out they had been wanting to get poetry on the air for a while, and they saw my recordings as a way to do it.

William Carlos Williams said, "If it ain't a pleasure, it ain't a poem." I try to keep his words in mind when I introduce poems; the idea is to open doors, not give reading instructions—to show just how pleasurable hearing and reading poems can be. The poems are often short, often accessible, showing that accessibility can be emotionally and intellectually complex. That poetry doesn't have to wear priestly robes, speak in puzzles, smell like a rare and perfect rose, and float in the realm of ideas instead of walking firmly on the ground. The poetry showcase has been extraordinarily popular for listeners. Letters and e-mails have come in from all over the world, some with questions and comments, some to applaud, some to heckle, others to critique and complain, most wanting to know where they could get the book. One man wrote from a maximum security prison, sending along a small religious medallion. Don't send it back, he said, it won't get through the metal detector. I loved the thought that poetry on the radio could get past metal detectors and into maximum security prisons.

It's a paradox, because when you listen to a poem on the radio you may be chopping tomatoes at home, driving the afternoon car pool, or typing at the office, and it feels as if the poet is speaking directly to you, even though millions of people are listening to the poem at the same time. It's a way to experience and interact with the poem in a very personal way, providing an intimacy that is both communal and private.

Likewise, the poet is sitting alone in a glassed-in sound studio; his or her voice is digitized, and then miraculously reassembled through a fiber-optic cable and sent into the homes, workplaces, and car stereos of millions. These poems offer a series of private, individual voices speaking out in the public sphere, an alternative to the numbing, all too familiar language of public discourse, newspeak, and advertising. Historically, rather than an instrument to channel and transmit possibilities for love, trust, and peace, the radio has often been and continues to be a vehicle for the apostles of hate and fear, fundamentalism, fanaticism, racism, and other ideologies of intolerance. The sound of the voice, over the airwaves, in sermon and in song, as well as in poetry, has a commanding effect on the human psyche. The ear is an opening with a direct line to the brain and the heart. Unlike the mouth and the eyes, it never closes.

While the radio is often used as a tool to propagate a false unified majority, it can also be a way to show both community and difference within community. We're not used to hearing private voices speaking on private experiences over the air, in the public sphere. When poems are sandwiched in between news and the telling of world events, they are themselves news. Poems are either praise-songs or laments. The poems collected here lean more toward the former, a natural counterpoint to the news of lament: floods, war, business fraud, and political shenanigans that fill the airwaves. The poems often speak to what Paul Muldoon calls "the conditions of joy," a condition much underrepresented in the news and, it could be argued, in contemporary poetry. Often the poems are very funny, breaking down stereotypes that poetry has to be anguished and self-absorbed. Several poems look at the same experience from different angles and perspectives: for example, there are two poems that deal with the wisdom offered by a child to passengers on a jumbo jet flight. There are several poems about birth and several birthday poems; more than one poem takes place in a garden or graveyard; there are several praise poems to the body. There are poems about work, play, music, love, lovemaking, beginnings, endings, family, eating, drinking, gardening, shopping, spirituality, sports, legacies, naming, aging, politics, art, culture, city life, country life, travel, history. There are songs, odes, sonnets, instructions, litanies, prayers, lullabies, tributes, diatribes, blues, catalogues, praise-songs, and laments. All of the poems are marked by a deep attention to the world, be it attention to memory, music, emotion, or thought. They each have a pulse, a unique physical and spiritual presence, located in the school of the five senses, comfortable more with questions than answers, finding meaning in gaps, remnants, and silences as they traverse ad infinitum the commonplace, the other unnamable place, and that mysterious place in between.

In his great poem "Leaves of Grass," Walt Whitman writes about America's "Athletic Democracy," a democracy fueled by a deft, precise, agile imagination, with the ability to shift, spin, leap; to contain contradictions and multitudes. A democracy in which Whitman warned us to *resist much, obey little.* A democracy that is not based on conformity, but rather on unity through acknowledgment and celebration of difference. This ideal is at the heart of this collection.

Our greatest national illness is our isolation: an isolation that breeds fear, forcing us to live a life deprived of real intimacy. Fear breeds more fear, and the longer we live in isolation, the more we are vulnerable to the wiles of power-mongers and the more we are willing to engage in group-think, making sweeping generalizations about our neighbors. Poetry cuts through this isolation, as particular voices speak from particular backgrounds and experiences, refusing to generalize on the human experience.

I hope readers come to these poems with an openness, and can let go of trying to dissect or overanalyze. Instead, enjoy the surprising images and music of the imagination at play. To experience that music, read the poems out loud to yourself, to a friend, stranger, lover, or your dog. Try to feel comfortable with ambiguity, with not having all the answers, as did Keats, who advocated the concept of negative capability: to be able to live with uncertainty, mystery, doubt, without reaching after fact and reason. Or what the great Spanish poet Federico Garcia Lorca calls "Duende: a mysterious power which everyone senses and nobody explains."

The first poem in this book starts with a journey—Quincy Troupe's poem "Flight," taking us high above California's Pacific coastline—and the book ends with a journey, Elizabeth Spires' poem "On the Island," with a ferry pulling out into the Atlantic Ocean. In between there are many journeys across the terrains and frequencies of the human comedy, journeys into foreign countries that you have known since birth, where the fun is in getting lost and in being found. A trip that is both familiar and new, where the extraordinary becomes ordinary and vice versa. Please think of this book as an invitation, an imaginative challenge to respond, a taking off point, a meeting place, and a conversation.

> Stranger, if you're passing me and desire to speak to me,
>   why should you not speak to me?
> And why should I not speak to you?
>
> —*Walt Whitman*

CATHERINE BOWMAN
BLOOMINGTON, INDIANA
AUGUST 2002

WORD *of* MOUTH

QUINCY TROUPE

When Quincy Troupe was growing up in St. Louis in the 50s, family and friends expected him to become an athlete like his father, the great Negro League catcher, Quincy Troupe Sr. All that changed while he was in France playing basketball on an all-army team. That's where he met philosopher Jean-Paul Sartre, who advised Troupe to become a poet after reading some of his work. Since then Troupe has written more than sixteen volumes of poetry, fiction, and nonfiction. With Miles Davis he coauthored *Miles: The Autobiography*. For several years he held the World Heavyweight Poetry Championship at The Taos Poetry Circus. Troupe says his poetry comes out of the rhythms of the Baptist sermon, barbershop storytelling, and the rock, blues, and jazz he heard growing up (Chuck Berry lived down the street from him). Performance, the oral tradition, and the audience are essential elements of Troupe's poetry. He believes the poet should be part of the community, not an outsider—a singer of many tribal songs in the tradition of the ancient bards, the African-American preacher, and the African griot. He often collaborates and performs with jazz musicians and composers. His poems can be read in the way we might experience John Coltrane's or Jimi Hendrix's "Sheets of Sound." They are big canvases, "sound paintings" that invite us to participate in the process of their lush and dynamic making. In his work we hear how language and poetry become a vehicle for imaginative flight, an occasion to shape-shift and change dreams. In this imaginative flight Troupe refuses to accept the tyranny of the concrete.

FLIGHT

at sunset across a western horizon, bright mauves, oranges & purples
streak with pure speed of broomstrokes, in a glowing ed clark painting
that is a hamburger patty between buns of dark earth & sky

& the pacific ocean stretched out there is a moment deep inside
history, is perhaps a man telling the world what his eyes do not see
where the coastline of california is a necklace of pearls

& diamonds roped like a noose around throats of harbors beneath
the oozing night, spreading now, from top to bottom
like a squid's amoeba ink, or whatever our vision imagines

there, now, the light sinking fast past canada & alaska to the north
& swallowed whole there in the fish mouth of the pacific, where the sun
is replaced by the vision of a ping-pong ball sticking to the wet black wall

of a room freshly painted & it looks like the moon positioning itself there
outside this airplane window, its mysterious, ghost white face centered
inside our imaginations, where winds seem still but blow fierce

as the jet-stream tongue of a great poet's blowtorch breath
fires cadences of looping saxophone miracles deep into our lives
stretch them into lines where heartbeats are caesuras

arresting speech in the middle of a sentence, like a glorious sunrise
back in the east, at dawn, stops us in our tracks, light there suddenly
breaking the darkness, pure & sweet as a baby's sweet breath

EYE CHANGE DREAMS

for Joe Overstreet, Corrine Jennings & George Lewis

eye change dreams at 42nd street, times square
as swirling people wearing technicolor attitudes speed
through packed days, carrying speech that machine-guns out
in rhythms equaling movement of averted stares
squares even sashay by quick in flip
mimicking motions, as slick street hustlers roll their eyes around
like marbles searching for hits, lick their chops after clicking onto
some slow-witted hicks dribbling spit down their lips
eating hot dogs paid with fifty-dollar bills
in broad daylight—

                                          yeah, tell me about it, trick—

escalator sidewalks moving everything along
so swiftly everyone thinks it's their own feet carrying
           their bodies, grooving to a different song
                       than say, in gloster, mississippi

where time is a turtle moving after a flood has crawled back
into the space it came out of in the first place
hear no beepers here
in gloster, no portable telephones panicking anywhere
only the constant slow humming glide of bloated mosquitoes
as they slide through air & bank in for fresh blood-kills
               wind-tongue guiding them into the target
                     wobbling on their zigzag ride above bearded

irises waving sword-shaped leaves in the breeze
as if preparing to do righteous battle with anyone or something
like people living in the big apple (their game faces constantly in place—
& they even wear them into bathrooms, so scared to death they are
of running into some cold-blooded rat there

staking out their own notion of territorial space)
try keeping their fluctuating dreams up to speed
switching up each & every moment, in midtown manhattan,
        manic chameleons
everywhere, here, changing faces at high noon, say,
on 42nd street & 8th avenue, claustrophobic
heat-drenching crowds packed in, in august, locks in on flesh cold
as a triple life sentence served out at comstock—
people here switching up gears, trying to sidestep panic
                in the middle of slapstick dreams
                        & in the center of it all

a con man who looks like swifty lazar, the late hollywood agent,
tools around inside a white rolls royce, peddling gimmicks for old
        false-tooth legends,
who look so bizarre in public devoid of heavy makeup—
comic, even—outside of their dream machines, illusions—
tattered memorabilia the con man peddles at some tacky bazaar
inside a rundown building, in a cobwebbed room, where he hawks
        fading photographs of
zsa zsa gabor in her prime, before she started breaking down
in front of our eyes, wearing all that weird graphic white
pancake makeup over her everchanging face-lifts, masking the dreams
we wear ourselves, inside our switching, ballistic imaginations
bewitching us here as we move through times square
popping with the charge of electrical currents

energy eye imagined this poem having when eye first started writing it
than having to deal with how it slowed down midway through,
when eye hit that part about gloster, a third of the way down,
& tried to avoid all those zigzagging mosquitoes
divebombing in for fresh blood-kills—
my direction moving all over the place after that, changing up the focus,
the rhythm, the way my dipstick lines started composing themselves—

at that point in time, they began making it all up
as they went along, as if they were different musicians improvising
this poem—like the swifty lazar look-alike peddling old hollywood
wonders before the fall, before they became toothless legends,
before they became zsa zsa gabor

this sputnik verbal drumstick—a thing to be eaten
after all—promises way more than it could ever deliver
traveling at the speed of complete bullshit, as it were—

a technicolored times-square attitude, without rhyme,
riding in on a broomstick, heartsick & caustic

homesick for that good old big-apple charge

CZESLAW MILOSZ

Nobel Laureate Czeslaw Milosz was born in Lithuania in 1911. He has lived in California for many years, where he teaches Slavic languages at the University of California, Berkeley. He says he was born and grew up on the very borderline between Rome and Byzantium. Many of his poems are journeys over borderlines, mystical mappings across geography and time. His poems are full of open space and flight. He also thinks of himself as a realist, a great believer in what can be directly perceived by the five senses. Milosz was a young poet in Warsaw when it was occupied by the Nazis. It was there Milosz saw, in the face of chaos and destruction, that a poetry of hope was as essential as bread and water for survival. Poetry, according to Milosz, rises out of the remnants of ruins. He says he has never taught poetry writing because he doesn't know how his poems come about. He thinks they are dictated to him by some kind of *daimon*—a divine power or spirit. As a child, he wanted to be a naturalist, or more specifically, a specialist in birds, but he changed his mind because he thought nature was too cruel. Milosz describes what he hopes the poetry of the future will be: "The rhythm of the body will be in it, heartbeat, pulse, sweating, menstrual flow, the gluiness of sperm, the squatting position at urinating, the movements of the intestines, together with the sublime needs of the spirit, and our duality will find its form in it, without renouncing one zone or the other." He calls "Preparation" a poem of sarcasm toward the twentieth century.

PREPARATION

Still one more year of preparation.
Tomorrow at the latest I'll start working on a great book
In which my century will appear as it really was.
The sun will rise over the righteous and the wicked.
Springs and autumns will unerringly return,
In a wet thicket a thrush will build his nest lined with clay
And foxes will learn their foxy natures.

And that will be the subject, with addenda. Thus: armies
Running across frozen plains, shouting a curse
In a many-voiced chorus; the cannon of a tank
Growing immense at the corner of a street; the ride at dusk
Into a camp with watchtowers and barbed wire.

No, it won't happen tomorrow. In five or ten years.
I still think too much about the mothers
And ask what is man born of woman.
He curls himself up and protects his head
While he is kicked by heavy boots; on fire and running,
He burns with bright flame; a bulldozer sweeps him into a clay pit.
Her child. Embracing a teddy bear. Conceived in ecstasy.

I haven't learned yet to speak as I should, calmly.

With not-quite truth
and not-quite art
and not-quite law
and not-quite science

Under not-quite heaven
on the not-quite earth
the not-quite guiltless
and the not-quite degraded

A SONG ON THE END OF THE WORLD

On the day the world ends
A bee circles a clover,
A fisherman mends a glimmering net.
Happy porpoises jump in the sea,
By the rainspout young sparrows are playing
And the snake is gold-skinned as it should always be.

On the day the world ends
Women walk through the fields under their umbrellas,
A drunkard grows sleepy at the edge of a lawn,
Vegetable peddlers shout in the street
And a yellow-sailed boat comes nearer the island,
The voice of a violin lasts in the air
And leads into a starry night.

And those who expected lightning and thunder
Are disappointed.
And those who expected signs and archangels' trumps
Do not believe it is happening now.
As long as the sun and the moon are above,
As long as the bumblebee visits a rose,
As long as rosy infants are born
No one believes it is happening now.

Only a white-haired old man, who would be a prophet
Yet is not a prophet, for he's much too busy,
Repeats while he binds his tomatoes:
There will be no other end of the world,
There will be no other end of the world.

Warsaw, 1944

IN COMMON

What is good? Garlic. A leg of lamb on a spit.
Wine with a view of boats rocking in a cove.
A starry sky in August. A rest on a mountain peak.

What is good? After a long drive water in a pool and a sauna.
Lovemaking and falling asleep, embraced, your legs touching hers.
Mist in the morning, translucent, announcing a sunny day.

I am submerged in everything that is common to us, the living.
Experiencing this earth for them, in my flesh.
Walking past the vague outline of skyscrapers? anti-temples?
In valleys of beautiful, though poisoned, rivers.

HEATHER McHUGH

Heather McHugh says she comes from a long line of punsters. Her poetry is witty and intellectual, full of wordplay and linguistic hijinks. It is also very physical—full of the stuff of the world. For McHugh, everything becomes an occasion for insight—in one poem she writes about a child mesmerized by the light as 350 people watch *Lethal Weapon 3* on a jumbo jet circling Spokane. The secret life of writing, as she calls it, allows her to time travel back to a sixteenth-century salon, to share anatomical drawings with Titian, or to weave in the intricacies of Oriki song-makers. Even though her poems are in love with the world and the word, her work is never sentimental—McHugh says one of her main goals when writing is to leech the sugar out of every poem. McHugh calls "What He Thought" a poem of moral education, where the speaker experiences a profound change. She says, "Everyone claims to know, when one finally realizes in a mindboggling way wisdom is the relinquishing of our need to know." She believes the author must constantly undermine and mine her own sense of authority. The tools for this task: the imagination and a dictionary.

THE SIZE OF SPOKANE

The baby isn't cute. In fact he's
a homely little pale and headlong
stumbler. Still, he's one
of us—the human beings
stuck on flight 295 (Chicago to Spokane);
and when he passes my seat twice
at full tilt this then that direction,
I look down from Lethal Weapon 3 to see
just why. He's

running back and forth
across a sunblazed circle on
the carpet—something brilliant, fallen
from a porthole. So! it's light
amazing him, it's only light, despite
some three and one
half hundred
people, propped in rows
for him to wonder at; it's light
he can't get over, light he can't
investigate enough, however many
zones he runs across it,
flickering himself.

The umpteenth time
I see him coming, I've had
just about enough; but then
he notices me noticing and stops—
one fat hand on my armrest—to
inspect the oddities of me.

*

Some people cannot hear.
Some people cannot walk.
But everyone was
sunstruck once, and set adrift.
Have we forgotten how
astonishing this is? so practiced all our senses
we cannot imagine them? foreseen instead of seeing
all the all there is? Each spectral port,
each human eye

is shot through with a hole, and everything we know
goes in there, where it feeds a blaze. In a flash

the baby's old; Mel Gibson's hundredth comeback seems
less clever; all his chases and embraces
narrow down, while we
fly on (in our
plain radiance of vehicle)

toward what cannot stay small forever.

WHAT HE THOUGHT
for Fabbio Doplicher

We were supposed to do a job in Italy
and, full of our feeling for
ourselves (our sense of being
Poets from America) we went
from Rome to Fano, met
the mayor, mulled
a couple matters over (what's
cheap date, they asked us; what's
flat drink). Among Italian literati

we could recognize our counterparts:
the academic, the apologist,
the arrogant, the amorous,
the brazen and the glib—and there was one

administrator (the conservative), in suit
of regulation gray, who like a good tour guide
with measured pace and uninflected tone narrated
sights and histories the hired van hauled us past.
Of all, he was most politic and least poetic,
so it seemed. Our last few days in Rome
(when all but three of the New World Bards had flown)
I found a book of poems this
unprepossessing one had written: it was there
in the *pensione* room (a room he'd recommended)
where it must have been abandoned by
the German visitor (was there a bus of *them?*)
to whom he had inscribed and dated it a month before.
I couldn't read Italian, either, so I put the book
back into the wardrobe's dark. We last Americans

were due to leave tomorrow. For our parting evening then
our host chose something in a family restaurant, and there
we sat and chatted, sat and chewed,
till, sensible it was our last
big chance to be poetic, make
our mark, one of us asked

                       "What's poetry?
Is it the fruits and vegetables and
marketplace of Campo dei Fiori, or
the statue there?" Because I was

the glib one, I identified the answer
instantly, I didn't have to think—"The truth
is both, it's both," I blurted out. But that
was easy. That was easiest to say. What followed
taught me something about difficulty,
for our underestimated host spoke out,
all of a sudden, with a rising passion, and he said:

The statue represents Giordano Bruno,
brought to be burned in the public square
because of his offense against
authority, which is to say
the Church. His crime was his belief
the universe does not revolve around
the human being: God is no
fixed point or central government, but rather is
poured in waves through all things. All things
move. "If God is not the soul itself, He is
the soul of the soul of the world." Such was
his heresy. The day they brought him
forth to die, they feared he might
incite the crowd (the man was famous

for his eloquence). And so his captors
placed upon his face
an iron mask, in which

he could not speak. That's
how they burned him. That is how
he died: without a word, in front
of everyone.
                And poetry—
                           (we'd all
put down our forks by now, to listen to
the man in gray; he went on
softly)—
                poetry is what

he thought, but did not say.

UNGUENT

Instead of angels, give us aero-
gels. Diaphanous as surfaces of soap,

lightest of the solids on this earth,
an aerogel won't burn, beneath our most
insistent blowtorch. We created it to be
a lightweight indestructibility,
just as we did (in good
old days) our bombs, and just
as in the good old days, we'll sell
a bit of it to you. Just take

our word for it, it's better
than the gist of gism, better than the best

of bed. Directly out of it will come
the aero-arrows of idea, which lead
to speech balloons and quick ignition pens.
Between the coupled wars, and times, and causes, prime
seems fed up, misled, laid. A thought

is nothing but a need
for energy, a body's mission: be
suggestive to a head. Instead of angels,

give us urges. We'll take over, if the mover's dead.

HIGH JINX

Either they treed me, or I hid
in the weed, or wash
was my overcoat, or drink
was my wish. Either they missed

my face in the tea, or my stink
in the hash, or my hand
in the honeysuckle. I've been wanted
seven years, and wasted more; been

burned, interred. Either they didn't
fertilize me, or I turned
to a desert rat; either I jumped ship
or they dumped me; I was game

or they shot my pool
with lily-killer. Man. Either you
used up your stunt juice or
my antibody grew.

CAMPBELL McGRATH

Campbell McGrath makes music out of the noise of our times, by making poetry out of what is often considered "unpoetic." Rubbing poetry's oversoul and underbelly, he writes about American landscape, history, and society, and analyzes and celebrates its cultures both high and low. In fact, he says, "The distinction between high culture and low culture is a false one—like the distinction between poetry and prose." He writes poems about Elvis, Las Vegas, *People Magazine*, microwave burritos at the 7-11, Costco, Bob Hope, rock and roll, and the bars of Manhattan and Chicago. Many of his poems are inspired by road trips across the country. Following in the tradition of Walt Whitman, William Carlos Williams, and Woody Guthrie, McGrath celebrates and critiques America's brilliance and absurdities. Since the beginning, poets have loved to name, catalogue, and list. Emerson calls the poet a namer, the true doctor that turns the world to glass. In "Delphos, Ohio," McGrath revels in and meditates on the overabundance of names across the American trajectory and what those names imply when thinking about naming his own child.

DELPHOS, OHIO

is where we turned around, surrendered to fate, gave in to defeat and
abandoned our journey at a town with three stoplights, one good mechanic
and a name of possibly oracular significance.

Which is how we came to consider calling the baby Delphos.

Which is why we never made it to Pennsylvania, never arrived to help J.B.
plant trees on the naked mountaintop he calls a farm, never hiked down the
brush-choked trail for groceries in the gnomic hamlet of Mann's Choice,
never hefted those truckloads of bundled bodies nor buried their delicate
rootling toes in the ice and mud of rocky meadows.

Blue spruce, black walnut, white pine, silver maple.

And that name! Mann's Choice. Finger of individual will poked in the face
of inexorable destiny.

Which is how we came to consider calling the baby Hamlet, Spruce or
Pennsylvania.

But we didn't make it there. Never even got to Lima or Bucyrus, let alone
Martin's Ferry, let alone West Virginia, let alone the Alleghenies tumbled
across the state line like the worn-out molars of a broken-down plow horse
munching grass in a hayfield along the slate grey Juniata.

Because the engine balked.

Because the shakes kicked in and grew like cornstalks hard as we tried to
ignore them, as if we could push that battered blue Volvo across the wintry
heart of the Midwest through sheer determination.

Which is foolish.

And the man in Delphos told us so.

Fuel injector, he says. Can't find even a sparkplug for foreign cars in these parts. Nearest dealer would be Toledo or Columbus, or down the road in Fort Wayne.

Which is Indiana. Which is going backwards.

Which is why they drive Fords in Ohio.

Which is how we came to consider calling the baby Edsel, Henry, Pinto or Sparks.

Which is why we spent the last short hour of evening lurching and vibrating back through those prosperous bean fields just waiting for spring to burst the green-shingled barns of Van Wert County.

Which is how we came to consider calling the baby Verna, Daisy, Persephone or Soy.

By this time we're back on the freeway, bypassing beautiful downtown Fort Wayne in favor of the rain forest at Exit 11, such is the cognomen of this illuminated Babel, this litany, this sculptural aviary for neon birds, these towering aluminum and tungsten weeds,

bright names raised up like burning irons to brand their sign upon the heavens.

Exxon, Burger King, Budgetel, Super 8.

Which is how we came to consider calling the baby Bob Evans.

Which is how we came to consider calling the baby Big Boy, Wendy, Long John Silver or Starvin' Marvin.

Which is how we came to salve our wounds by choosing a slightly better than average motel, and bringing in the Colonel to watch "Barnaby Jones" while Elizabeth passes out quick as you like

leaving me alone with my thoughts and reruns

in the oversized bed of an antiseptic room on an anonymous strip of indistinguishable modules among the unzoned outskirts of a small mid-western city named for the Indian killer Mad Anthony Wayne.

Which is why I'm awake at 4 A.M. as the first trucks sheet their thunder down toward the interstate.

Which is when I feel my unborn child kick and roll within the belly of its sleeping mother, three heartbeats in two bodies, two bodies in one blanket, one perfect and inviolable will like a flower preparing to burst into bloom,

and its aurora lights the edge of the window like nothing I've ever seen.

CAPITALIST POEM #42

While Elizabeth shops at Costco, Sam and I play hide & seek
among the bales and pallets in that vast warehouse of pure things.
Believe me, what little we do buy—napkins and pain killers,
loops of figs, loose cashews, a carton of over-ripe cantaloupes,
tubs of discount laundry detergent and the Ansel Adams desk calendar,
three dozen lightbulbs, twenty-two metric socket wrenches,
tinkertoys, tea bags, tennis balls, Christmas tinsel,

frozen eggrolls and midget palm trees, string cheese, soda crackers
and computer software—is as nothing to what we leave behind,
the merest anthill against the Great Pyramid of Cheops,
a sidewalk crevice compared to that Grand Canyon of commodities.
Bright laughter, summer skies. So they descend into the abyss.

THE GOLDEN ANGEL PANCAKE HOUSE

Or coming out of Bento on a wild midwinter
midnight, or later, closing time Ron says, the last
rack of pool balls ratcheted down until dawn,
bottles corked and watered, lights out, going out
the door beneath the El tracks over Clark and Sheffield,
always a train showing up just then, loud, sure
as hell showering sparks upon the snowfall,
shaking slightly the lights and trestles, us
in our fellowship shouting and scurrying
like the more sprightly selves we once inhabited
behind parked cars and street signs, thinking,
hey, should we toss some snowballs? Bull's eye,
the beauty of fresh snow in the hands, like rubbing
tree-bark to catch that contact high direct
from the inexplicable source, unique however
often repeated, carried along on woolen thumbs
to the next absolutely necessary thing,
sloe gin fizzes to Green Mill jazz or the horror
of Jägermeister at the Ginger Man or
one of those German bars up around Irving Park
where a sup of the Weiss beer on tap is enough
to convince me to foreswear my stake in any vision
of the afterlife you might care to construct, say
the one with the photo of the owner in his Nazi

uniform beside a pristine fjord, could be Norway,
1940? Whichever, we're hungry now, cast out
into the false dawn of snow-coiffed streetlights
embowed like bowl-cut adolescents or
Roman emperors sated on frost, thumbs up
or down to hash & eggs at Manny's
or the locally infamous Alps, then there's one
at which I never ate though it looked absolutely
irreplaceable, the Golden Angel Pancake House,
which is a poem by Rilke I've never read
though I've used its restroom, seen its dim
celestial figures like alien life-forms
in a goldfish bowl, tasted its lonely nectar
in every stack of silver dollar buttermilk flapjacks,
though the food, for all I know, is unutterably
awful, the way it resonates is what carries me
down the swirled chords of memory
toward the bottom of the frosted glass
aquarium of dreams, whatever that means, it's
what it meant to me coming home those nights
from the Lutheran college after teaching
the *Duino Elegies* to the daughters and sons
of Minnesota farmers, the footbridge over
the North Branch of the Chicago River, frozen
solid, eddies of whirling ionized powder
around my boots in the bone-cold subzero
that makes the lights in the windows of houses
so painfully beautiful—is it the longing
to get the hell inside or the tears the wind
inevitably summons forth? Homeward,
all the way down Lincoln Avenue's amazing
arabesques and ethnic configurations
of Korean babushkas and Croatian karaoke
that feeling set upon me like the overture to god

knows what dread disease, that cathartic, lustral,
yes, idiot laughter, threat of tears in the gullet,
adam's apple stringing its yoyo to follow
the bouncing ball, as if boulevards of such purity
could countenance no science but eudaemonics,
hardly likely, as if this promethean eruption
were merely one of the more colorful dog-
and-pony acts of simple happiness, acrobatic
dromedaries or narcoleptic dancing bears,
but which I've come to see with perfect hindsight
was no less than the mighty strongman
joy himself bending bars of steel upon a tattooed
skull, so much nobler and more rapacious
than his country cousins, bliss, elation, glee,
a troupe of toothless, dipsomaniacal clowns,
multiform and variable as flurries from blizzards,
while joy is singular, present tense, predatory, priapic,
paradoxically composed of sorrow and terror
as ice is made of water, dense and pure,
darkly bejewelled, music rather than poetry,
preliterate, lapidary, dumb as an ox, cruel as youth,
magnificent and remorseless as Chicago in winter.

THE GULF

Floating in the gulf, on a hot June day, listening to the seashells sing.

Eyes open I watch their migrations, their seismic shifts and tidal seizures, as I am seized and lifted, lulled and hushed and serenaded. Eyes closed, I drift amid their resonant sibilance, soft hiss and crackle in the tide wash, ubiquitous underwater, a buzz like static, or static electricity—but not mechanical—organic and musical, metallic as casino muzak, piles of change raked together, a handful of pennies down a child's slide. Eyes open I see them rise as one with the water, climbing the ridge with the incoming surge and then, released, called back, slide slowly down the face of their calcified escarpment, the sandy berm the small rippling waves butt up against and topple over—flop, whoosh—a fine wash of shells and shell bits and shards, a slurry of coquinas and scallops and sunrays, coral chunks, tubes and frills, the volute whorls of eroded whelks, a mass of flinty chips and nacreous wafers, singing as it descends. Like mermaids, singing. But not a song. Stranger and more varied, more richly textured, many-timbred, Gregorian hymns or aboriginal chanting, the music of pygmies in a forest clearing, complex, symphonic, indecipherable. But not human. Elemental. Like rain. Bands of tropical rain approaching from the jungle, sweeping the tile verandah, the sheet metal roof, against the slats of the louvered window and across the floor of storm light and coffee-flavored dust—but not liquid—mineral—mountains of shattered porcelain, broken bottles en route to the furnace—but not glass and not rain and not even a rain of glass. Ice. The day after the ice storm, when the sun peeks out, and wind comes off the lake, and what has so beautifully jeweled the trees all morning breaks loose in a sequence of tumbling cascades, chiming like tumbrels and lost castanets, falling upon snow-covered cars and encrusted fences, discarded Christmas trees piled up in the alley, smelling of wet balsam, string and plastic in their hair, and for-gotten tinsel, and every needle encased in a fine translucent sheath of ice, and as I reach to touch them my fingers brush the sand and my knees bump the bottom and I am called back with a start, alien, suspended, wholly conceived within that other music, body in the water like the water in the flesh and the liquid in the crystal and the crystal in the snowflake and the mind within the body like the branch within its skin of ice.

Eyes open. Eyes closed.

Floating in the gulf, listening to seashells, thinking of the Christmas trees in the back-alleys of Chicago.

C. D. WRIGHT

C. D. Wright's poems echo with the wit and wisdom and the cadences of the Ozark Mountains where she was born and raised. She grew up around towns named Ben Hur, Greasy Corner, and Okay, and her lines are filled with the vernacular of that landscape: the music of blues, old men, chain saws, cornfields, crawdads, pimento cheese sandwiches, and fabric gardenias. The daughter of a judge and a court reporter, she once wrote that her line of work, poetry, "beats the bejesus out of a gig as gizzard-splitter at the processing plant or cleaning up a leak at the germ warfare center." Her poems are inhabited by friendly and unfriendly spirits; decay and growth; order and chaos. Each poem is a place where affliction is soothed by the cool rain of the heart.

EVERYTHING GOOD BETWEEN
MEN AND WOMEN

has been written in mud and butter
and barbecue sauce. The walls and
the floors used to be gorgeous.
The socks off-white and a near match.
The quince with fireblight
but we get two pints of jelly
in the end. Long walks strengthen
the back. You with a fever blister
and myself with a sty. Eyes
have we and we are forever prey
to one another's teeth. The torrents
go over us. Thunder has not harmed
anyone we know. The river coursing
through us is dirty and deep. The left
hand protects the rhythm. Watch
your head. No fires should be
unattended. Especially when wind. Each
receives a free swiss army knife.
The first few tongues are clearly
preparatory. The impression
made by yours I carry to my grave. It is
just so sad so creepy so beautiful.
Bless it. We have so little time
to learn, so much. . . . The river
courses dirty and deep. Cover the lettuce.
Call it a night. O soul. Flow on. Instead.

SONG OF THE GOURD

In gardening I continued to sit on my side of the car: to drive whenever possible at the usual level of distraction: in gardening I shat nails glass contaminated dirt and threw up on the new shoots: in gardening I learned to praise things I had dreaded: I pushed the hair out of my face: I felt less responsible for one man's death one woman's long-term isolation: my bones softened: in gardening I lost nickels and ring settings I uncovered buttons and marbles: I lay half the worm aside and sought the rest: I sought myself in the bucket and wondered why I came into being in the first place: in gardening I turned away from the television and went around smelling of offal the inedible parts of the chicken: in gardening I said excelsior: in gardening I required no company I had to forgive my own failure to perceive how things were: I went out barelegged at dusk and dug and dug and dug: I hit rock my ovaries softened: in gardening I was protean as in no other realm before or since: I longed to torch my old belongings and belch a little flame of satisfaction: in gardening I longed to stroll farther into soundlessness: I could almost forget what happened many swift years ago in arkansas: I felt like a god from down under: chthonian: in gardening I thought this is it body and soul I am home at last: excelsior: praise the grass: in gardening I fled the fold that supported the war: only in gardening could I stop shrieking: stop: stop the slaughter: only in gardening could I press my ear to the ground to hear my soul let out an unyielding noise: my lines softened: I turned the water onto the joy-filled boychild: only in gardening did I feel fit to partake to go on trembling in the last light: I confess the abject urge to weed your beds while the bittersweet overwhelmed my daylilies: I summoned the courage to grin: I climbed the hill with my bucket and slept like a dipper in the cool of your body: besotted with growth; shot through by green

JACK GILBERT

Jack Gilbert grew up in Pittsburgh, the son of a circus worker, boot-legger, and detective who sold phony stocks and bonds. When Gilbert was named a Yale Younger Poet in 1961, he became an overnight sensation, a poetry glamour star, with full spreads in *Teen*, *Esquire*, and *Vogue*. Librarians told him his first collection *Views of Jeopardy* was one of the most stolen books in America. Over the years he became less and less interested in fame and in the lifestyle of the literati. After winning a Guggenheim fellowship, he left the United States and didn't publish again for seventeen years. He spent that time living a solitary life in Greece exploring his life's obsession: the lyric possibilities of love. He believes that romantic love is our species' greatest invention. In fact, Gilbert calls himself the only serious romantic he's ever met. Gilbert says the arts offer us a way to experience the world, "to understand with our body and eat with our mind."

TEAR IT DOWN

We find out the heart only by dismantling what
the heart knows. By redefining the morning,
we find a morning that comes just after darkness.
We can break through marriage into marriage.
By insisting on love we spoil it, get beyond
affection and wade mouth-deep into love.
We must unlearn the constellations to see the stars.
But going back toward childhood will not help.
The village is not better than Pittsburgh.
Only Pittsburgh is more than Pittsburgh.
Rome is better than Rome in the same way the sound
of raccoon tongues licking the inside walls
of the garbage tub is more than the stir
of them in the muck of the garbage. Love is not
enough. We die and are put into the earth forever.
We should insist while there is still time. We must
eat through the wildness of her sweet body already
in our bed to reach the body within that body.

ALMOST HAPPY

The goldfish is dead this morning on the bottom
of her world. The autumn sky is white,
the trees are coming apart in the cold rain.
Loneliness gets closer and closer.
He drinks hot tea and sings off-key:
This train ain't a going-home train, this train.
This is not a going-home train, this train.
This train ain't a going-home train 'cause
my home's on a gone-away train. That train.

MARRIED

I came back from the funeral and crawled
around the apartment, crying hard,
searching for my wife's hair.
For two months got them from the drain,
from the vacuum cleaner, under the refrigerator,
and off the clothes in the closet.
But after other Japanese women came,
there was no way to be sure which were
hers, and I stopped. A year later,
repotting Michiko's avocado, I find
a long black hair tangled in the dirt.

THE FORGOTTEN DIALECT
OF THE HEART

How astonishing it is that language can almost mean,
and frightening that it does not quite. *Love*, we say,
God, we say, *Rome* and *Michiko*, we write, and the words
get it wrong. We say *bread* and it means according
to which nation. French has no word for home,
and we have no word for strict pleasure. A people
in northern India is dying out because their ancient
tongue has no words for endearment. I dream of lost
vocabularies that might express some of what
we no longer can. Maybe the Etruscan texts would
finally explain why the couples on their tombs
are smiling. And maybe not. When the thousands
of mysterious Sumerian tablets were translated,
they seemed to be business records. But what if they
are poems or psalms? My joy is the same as twelve

Ethiopian goats standing silent in the morning light.
O Lord, thou art slabs of salt and ingots of copper,
as grand as ripe barley lithe under the wind's labor.
Her breasts are six white oxen loaded with bolts
of long-fibered Egyptian cotton. My love is a hundred
pitchers of honey. Shiploads of thuya are what
my body wants to say to your body. Giraffes are this
desire in the dark. Perhaps the spiral Minoan script
is not a language but a map. What we feel most has
no name but amber, archers, cinnamon, horses and birds.

DAVID LEHMAN

In 1996, poet, scholar, and teacher David Lehman gave himself an assignment. Following in a long tradition of poems that turn the genre of daybooks, diaries, and journals into poetic form, he decided to write a poem every single day for a year. Four years later, he took the best of those poems and compiled *The Daily Mirror*—named for a now-defunct New York City newspaper. He collected a second volume of his daily poems in *The Evening Sun*. Lehman's work shows how the quotidian events of life—a summer baseball game, a turkey club sandwich—can be both poetry and the "news." Because he writes a poem a day, poetry becomes part of everyday life, not some agonized, precious activity written in a lofty sphere. He demystifies the whole process. His poems "listen and talk at the same time." Part of the pleasure of reading these poems is being invited into someone's secret diary or journal. Yet the poems' highly crafted voice belies their sense of self-confession. They are light on their feet, like a Fred Astaire tap dance solo, full of wit, élan, polish, and formal ease, giving a sense of both artifice and true sentiment. He calls his poems little time capsules meant to burst forward into some unspecified future.

JANUARY 1 [1998]

Some people confuse inspiration with lightning
not me I know it comes from the lungs and air
you breathe it in you breathe it out it circulates
it's the breath of my being the wind across the face
of the waters yes but it's also something that comes
at my command like a turkey club sandwich
with a cup of split pea soup or like tones
from Benny Goodman's clarinet my clarinet
the language that never fails to respond
some people think you need to be pure of heart
not true it comes to the pure and impure alike
the patient and impatient the lovers the onanists
and the virgins you just need to be able to listen
and talk at the same time and you'll hear it like
the long-delayed revelation at the end of the novel
which turns out to be something simple a traumatic
moment that fascinated us more when it was only
a fragment an old song a strange noise a mistake
of hearing a phone that wouldn't stop ringing

MARCH 16 [1996]

The weather is on a lottery
system and I've lucked out two
Saturdays in a row it's warm
in Tampa where I want to eat
paella and smoke a cigar and
wonder if Tampax was invented
here I remember the year
my favorite song was "All of Me"

by Sinatra the phrase on everyone's
lips was "in your face" I wrote
odes to the nudes in Lee Friedlander's
photos the tropical tufts of pubic
hair and cheap alarm clocks
constantly going off as if time
were speeding up and the cabdriver
taking me to the airport said
I know you you're the guy who
played the doctor on *Love Boat*

APRIL 26 [1998]

When my father
said *mein Fehler*
I thought it meant
"I'm a failure"
which was my error
which is what
mein Fehler means
in German which
is what my parents
spoke at home

AUGUST 31 [2000]

Happy Anniversary

You've been together
thirty-nine months
do I think that's
significant I do why
thirty-nine is the number
of months you need to be
accident-free to erase
traffic violations from
your driving record it's
the number of lines
in a sestina the number
of "Steps" in Hitchcock's
dream of espionage with
the male and female leads
handcuffed together
overnight on the train
to the distant north

DECEMBER 29 [1997]

I spent a month writing love poems
to women I didn't know (see May 7),
women I had met for a whole half
hour (August 18), fictional characters,
composite dream-drenched figures,
and all for the pleasure of being
a French poet in prewar Paris, having
a Gauloise and an espresso on the run,

I had vast metaphors to make,
no sooner did I have an idea than
I would witness its fulfillment,
a tower or a bridge, and head on
to the next project and of course you
were there with me the whole time
though unnamed in the rain as if
nothing could be more romantic
than a shared umbrella

WANG PING

Born in Shanghai, Wang Ping came of age during the Cultural Revolution. She remembers books being hauled into the street for public burnings. At the risk of severe punishment, she would meet secretly with friends to exchange paperbacks. A smuggled copy of Hans Christian Andersen's *Fairy Tales* was more precious to her than gold. At fifteen, she went to live in the countryside as part of her "re-education." There she learned about farming, but she also learned a certain cunning, goodness, and directness from the country people that she said freed her spirit and eventually became part of her poetics. She went on to study English literature at the University of Beijing. She witnessed the risks surrounding poetry, during those days when poets were reformed, killed, or silenced. She also learned how poetry could save. She said it was the writing of poetry that saved her, when she came here as a student in 1985 without money or community and when her spiritual compass hit the magnetic field of the American dream, as she describes in the poem "No Sense of Direction." She read her poem "These Images" on *All Things Considered* to celebrate the first day of spring.

NO SENSE OF DIRECTION

So just like this . out of the plane at Kennedy . Destination Flushing address . no sense of direction . what? . a quarter for the pay phone . no . all her luggage . Twenty-five dollars and a dictionary . first night in basement . sleepless . indigestion of dreams . want to scream but . no . her sponsor upstairs . silent night . staring into space . no sense of direction . hover between awareness and loss . first month working to pay off the plane ticket . selling Chinese antiques . Fifth Avenue . leaves falling on the homeless blanket . on the golden canopy of the store . "Two Worlds" . Pizza for lunch . on the boss . first bite of cheese . throwing up on the boss' shoes . no sense of value . no brain for business . too stubborn to be a running dog . out of the store . out of the basement . out hunting for jobs . two restaurants . Flushing for weekend . midtown from Monday to Friday . first apartment room in Bay Ridge . $180 for rent . four hours underground . reading *Ulysses* in train . or dozing . rocking like a cradle . mother rocker . sleeping in class . sorry Shakespeare . tender mercies . full time school or get out of America . lost in Time Square . "Someone give me a quarter please" . no sense of direction . Malaysian Chinese landlady . dream of becoming a fashion designer . furious at the question if she was lonely . kicked out the next week . $250 a room at Elmhurst from a Taiwanese couple . can't afford it . divorced engineer offers to pay half . offers to take her to the Jersey mall . her nose pressed against the window . looking into the consuming world . "Buy whatever you want" . as if dreams come true . what's the price . enter her room at night and carry her into his bed . more offers . a home . a car . a marriage . a green card . he snoring . bad breath . stare into space . sleepless . indigestion of the soul . no sense of direction . sit staring at her hands . infected with athlete's foot . suddenly see them wet . teardrops . what? . no! . no time for pity . too proud to sell . move to Harlem . where she belongs . different root . same fate . $100 . through a Chinese girlfriend . married for green card . thought she could settle down for a while . but in the third week someone turned the key in the lock at midnight . the owner . no . the lover of the Chinese girl . back from an interview in San Francisco . sold for a hundred . no more girlfriend . not available . another offer . one night shelter and a screw . "stinky meat" she was told after the business . in the dark . long after . tongue in the cheek . no speech possible . suddenly she realizes . gradually I realize . so much need for love . no time for love . this awful thought . drifting in and out . make it stop . God is love . What? . no! . no God for Chinese . sick of belief . but this need for love . no money for love . that December afternoon . roaming along Fifth Avenue . a job . waitress . bus girl . cashier . a place to stay . a bowl of instant noodles . grabbing at the straw . nothing there . on to the next . in the December snow . no sense of direction . feelings dismissed . how she survived . but this roar . this voice in her skull . this need to be loved . falling on her face . in the first snow . tender mercies . in the December snow . in the unheated basement . Jackson Heights . first night . flooded bathroom . floating mattress . yeast infection . punishment for the sin . face in her hands . avoiding a curious rat . on the eve of the Chinese New . what? . no? . OK . on the eve of Christ . no? . what? . New Year? . Good God! . sorry . good heaven . no God for Chinese . New Year's Eve . a rat sitting on my face. waiting . silence . Big Apple rising . trumpets blowing . something wet in hands . hers probably . no one else around . except for the rat . dear rat . Happy New Year . phone ringing . her sponsor's call . "ungrateful beast" . telling the story of the Harlem apartment to a journalist . how can Chinese betray Chinese . shame . no more connection . she is on her own . she has been on her own . only pretending she has someone behind her . Big Apple rising . no more dreams . no head . no brain . no sense of direction . only sequences of the apartments . six . what? . ten . Good God . sorry . good heaven . memories fading . last stop Flushing address . life recycles . time compressed . fragments of names . being achieved silence . images incapable of repose . asserting like maddened . recognizable even burned into ashes . clinging to the threshold . one has to believe something . face in her hands . tender mercies . on New Year's Eve . no sense of direction . no direction .

OF FLESH & SPIRIT

I was a virgin till twenty-three, then always had more than one lover at the same time—all secret.

In China, people go to jail for watching porno videos while condoms and pills are given out free.

When I saw the first bra my mom made for me, I screamed and ran out in shame.

For a thousand years, women's bound feet were the most beautiful and erotic objects for Chinese. Tits and asses were nothing compared to a pair of three-inch "golden lotuses." They must have been crazy or had problems with their noses. My grandma's feet, wrapped day and night in layers of bandages, smelled like rotten fish.

The asshole in Chinese: the eye of the fart.

A twenty-five-year-old single woman worries her parents. A twenty-eight-year-old single woman worries her friends and colleagues. A thirty-year-old single woman worries her bosses. A thirty-five-year-old woman is pitied and treated as a sexual pervert.

The most powerful curse: fuck your mother, fuck your grandmother, fuck your great-grandmother of eighteen generations.

One day, my father asked my mother if our young rooster was mature enough to jump, meaning to "mate." I cut in before my mother answered: "Yes, I saw him jump onto the roof of the chicken coop." I was ten years old.

Women call menstruation "the old ghost," science books call it "the moon period," and refined people say "the moonlight is flooding the ditch."

My first lover vowed to marry me in America after he took my virginity. He had two kids and an uneducated wife, and dared not ask the police for a divorce. He took me to see his American Chinese cousin who was staying in the Beijing Hotel and tried to persuade his cousin to sponsor him to come to New York. But his cousin sponsored me instead. That's how I'm here and why he went back to his wife, still cursing me.

Chinese peasants call their wives: that one in my house; old Chinese intellectuals: the doll in a golden house; in socialist China, husbands and wives call each other "my lover."

The story my grandma never tired of telling was about a man who was punished for his greed and had to walk around with a penis hanging from his forehead.

We don't say "fall in love," but "talk love."

When I left home, my father told me: "never talk love before you're twenty-five years old." I waited till twenty-three. Well, my first lover was a married coward. My first marriage lasted a week. My husband slept with me once, and I never saw him again.

THESE IMAGES

Thus like swans,
wings wide open in the air,
when spring splashes lakes onto shores,
where in the woods,
wild ducks wheeling in pairs
for a love nest, and snakes,
after spring's first thunders,
slide forth from winter's fields,

when raccoons lose their minds
mating among maple leaves
in Quaker cemeteries,
and golden smoke rises
above cypress trees, their needles
aquiver with too much pollen,
when songs flow from lips
and bare feet welcome the embrace of sand,
where, under the tent of a white sheet,
eyes fall on the sea-drenched forehead
of the beloved,
when the church bell rings,
children dash through the lunchroom,
their jackets of tropical fruit and birds of paradise
against the concrete ground of P.S. 19,
where words are at stake
and thoughts immobilized,
where life shouts with joy
and being is beauty and love
no longer clings,
where senses quicken their steps
to enter hearts of things . . .

So simple, these images,
their recognition
is in our nature,
yet too often neglected,
our eyes already elsewhere.
It is beyond the gods
why we hold onto our sorrows
so long, and so stubborn.

JOSEPH BRODSKY

Joseph Brodsky received the Nobel Prize for Literature in 1987 and was named Poet Laureate of the United States in 1991. Born and raised in Russia, he left school at the age of fifteen. He taught himself English and Polish by translating the work of Milosz, Eliot, and Donne. In his memoir *Less than One* he describes working in a cannon factory, a hospital morgue, as a geologist, and in a camp near the Arctic Circle where he was sentenced to five years hard labor by the government. He came to live permanently in the U.S. in 1972. Brodsky defines his main theme as "mostly what time does to a man, how it chisels the man, how it sort of chips him away, and what is left." In his poems what is chipped away, torn, severed, and broken is remade through rhyme, meter, musical delight, wordplay, and wit. He often writes about separation—separation from home, country, loved ones, God. We see this in the three poems below from various perspectives. In one poem he defines love as "separation, and the solitude that goes with it." Notice how "Törnfallet" braids the particular to the infinite in a series of ever-widening concentric circles—beginning with the sphere of the eye, to the clover wreath, to the oval lake, to the planet Venus.

A SONG

I wish you were here, dear,
I wish you were here.
I wish you sat on the sofa
and I sat near.
The handkerchief could be yours,
the tear could be mine, chin-bound.
Though it could be, of course,
the other way around.

I wish you were here, dear,
I wish you were here.
I wish we were in my car,
and you'd shift the gear.
We'd find ourselves elsewhere,
on an unknown shore.
Or else we'd repair
to where we've been before.

I wish you were here, dear,
I wish you were here.
I wish I knew no astronomy
when stars appear,
when the moon skims the water
that sighs and shifts in its slumber.
I wish it were still a quarter
to dial your number.

I wish you were here, dear,
in this hemisphere,
as I sit on the porch
sipping a beer.
It's evening, the sun is setting;

boys shout and gulls are crying.
What's the point of forgetting
if it's followed by dying?

BLUES

Eighteen years I've spent in Manhattan.
The landlord was good, but he turned bad.
A scumbag, actually. Man, I hate him.
Money is green, but it flows like blood.

I guess I've got to move across the river.
New Jersey beckons with its sulphur glow.
Say, numbered years are a lesser evil.
Money is green, but it doesn't grow.

I'll take away my furniture, my old sofa.
But what should I do with my windows' view?
I feel like I've been married to it, or something.
Money is green, but it makes you blue.

A body on the whole knows where it's going.
I guess it's one's soul that makes one pray,
even though above it's just a Boeing.
Money is green, and I am gray.

TÖRNFALLET

There is a meadow in Sweden
where I lie smitten,
eyes stained with clouds'
white ins and outs.

And about that meadow
roams my widow
plaiting a clover
wreath for her lover.

I took her in marriage
in a granite parish.
The snow lent her whiteness,
a pine was a witness.

She'd swim in the oval
lake whose opal
mirror, framed by bracken,
felt happy, broken.

And at night the stubborn
sun of her auburn
hair shone from my pillow
at post and pillar.

Now in the distance
I hear her descant.
She sings "Blue Swallow,"
but I can't follow.

The evening shadow
robs the meadow
of width and color.
It's getting colder.

As I lie dying
here, I'm eyeing
stars. Here's Venus;
no one between us.

PAUL BEATTY

When Paul Beatty read his work not long ago in San Diego, one young high school football player was so moved he vowed to give up his cleats and become a poet. Beatty's poems mostly comment on contemporary culture and urban life as they twist and turn down the page with full-throttle energy and linguistic verve. He started writing poetry in graduate school where he was working on a degree in psychology. He says what gave him the courage to focus on his writing full-time was seeing a Spike Lee film one semester. It wasn't so much the content of the film, he says, but the fact that a young African-American man was doing something creative that was being accepted by the mainstream. His highly crafted poems deploy a poetics of collage, zigzagging syncopation, and linguistic agility to praise and lampoon contemporary culture, juxtaposing elements of rap and jazz, colloquial speech and dialogue, comic book quotes, Shakespeare, and TV jingles. Through his structure, style, and economy of expression he offers a moral stance, a way of being in the world that celebrates lightness, motion, and skill.

Aa Bb Cc...Xx Yy and Zzing

will all the zoobelee zoo
elementary school teachers freeze

and stop chestizin me
with this *we hold these truths to be self evident* b.s.
            cuz i got as much chance of being president
            as one of ling lings dc panda cubs
                        livin to see three days of spring

DIB DAB

smooth as . . .

a baby nicholas brother
tap dancin in a porcelain tub
mr bubble suds
aye que lindo palms filled
with cocoa butter lotion

smooth as . . .

michael jordan
in the middle of his fifth
airborne freeze frame pump fake
a funky millionaire marionette
pissin on physics
his glossy fresh out the pacific
sea lion brown skin limbs
draped in 8th century heian kimono silk

smooth as . . .

sarah vaughan
holdin a note dipped in bronze
spit shined with a lonely bootblacks jukebox drool
buffed with chamois cloth and heartache

smooth as . . .

tap beer after midnight mass

smooth as . . .

wilma rudolph haulin ass through rome
long tennessee tigerbelle strides
walkin down gossamer winged myths
busted shackles in her wake
1960 runaway

smooth as . . .

an eric dolphy jazz workshopped
alto free swingin lead
that lets mingus know
where he can shove that bow
if he dont ease up pluckin pizzicato
over his solo

smooth as . . .

billy dee williams   nevermind

smooth as . . .

lady kung fu
flyin roof to roof

dealing five finger drunken monkey style tiger fisted death
to the imperialist aggressors
spinning heel roundhouse
hong kong backlot snap kick sound effects
a buttlength ponytail
trailing the action with a mind of its own

smooth as . . .

the first latin black korean
national hockey league offensive superstar
center ice crossovers
one hand on the stick
blue line breakaway
blastin a drive high and tight
stick side
red light and siren

smooth as . . .

granddads 30 year old
one sunday a month
white patent leather shoes
ones he wears with his lucky powder blue slacks
when he takes you to the track
santa anita belmont yonkers
gives you two disability dollars a race
and tells you to bet the trifecta
on the horses with the names you like

smooth as . . .

a cab calloway blip blap big band stikkle tat riff
rolling over his process

from front to back
sliding on its knees
down the greased part
of a geechee ghetto trickster in full regalia

smooth as fuck

AT EASE

every morning roundabout nine
the east 2nd street
red fire engines whine

    a shrill drill sergeant
    rousting my mind

        its time to rise and shine   shine
in the east village
another dollar draft recruit
    boot camp saloon sambo
        a genesee on tap dancin hambone poet

bivouacs in the groovy lower east side barracks
makin friends wid homespun poet pundit bums
constantly recitin jack kerouac

and for fun i attend
allnight outdoor open mikes
free readings about real people
who seem so lifelike

    last night i bought a stolen bike
    a freewheel three speed
    grew a goatee

camped out on avenue B
and for a change in perspective
went to   A Retrospective of Scatological Abstraction:
                        from Popeye to Gillespie

                        skeeter ta rebop rap pap debose
                                        debang
                                        deboom

                        i yam what i yam
                        and thats all that i yam
b'diddly bop repetitious rot
dont forget to stop at my seddity sop co-op
                        listen to my loizada
                                lambada
                                tostada
cholesterol-free blah blah blah poppycock

                                salt free nuts
                                salt free nuts

i just kickback n watch
black combat boots
move thru an east village tour of duty
                        an in unison death march
                                to the cadence
of the ultra cool

hop hop who
hut-hop hep who
hut-hop hep who
hut-hop het who
                eeney meany miney moe
                lets go back and write some more

i admit theres an urge
to merge ginsbergs
ice age incantations
with some inspired spitfire monk vibes

                    but no tai chi for me "g"
                    nix on the tye dye

          wont hindu my blues nor
                              tofu my soulfood
im gonna be
    the bulimic bohemian

                        eatin up my people
                        then purgin their regurgitated words
                        on the page
                                    and the poems
                                    become self made
                        little icarus birds
              immaculately hatched
from the multicultural nest eggs
of the east village and west l.a.
                          born to sing lyric segues
                while caged
whats the   latin
                  scientific
                        slave name
for pretty peacocks
      whose feathers span the flesh spectrum
                          but are stuck on with wax
it looks nice
but can it fly

look up in the sky
itsa bat
itsa crow
no its supernigger / indian / chicano / womanist / gay / asian everything

able to fly through the peephole
in the white medias ozone
          talk proper on the phone   and act ethnic at home

y know
its like multiculturalisms
the lefts right guard
of truth justice and the american way
              a spray-on deodorant
           against the stench of isms
              Contents under
              extreme pressure.
              May explode.

i understand the effort to prevent skin cancer
by removin epithets and fluorocarbons from the history texts

but multiculturalisms
sunblock jargon
        doesnt protect
        against big brother sun rays
        on days when niggas went to the beach and wore socks

to cover up the lack of respect for the blackfeet

  not the indians
        but the crusty lizard skin
        two inch thick toenailed

curled hammertoes
knuckled corns *my soul is rested* on

never heard anyone
other than
a black man
utter these words   *man she got some pretty feet*

dont nobody appreciate feet
like we do

i fell in love with my second grade teachers feet
her toes smooth n flat   her insteps were all that
i would drop my pencil a lot
to watch her wiggle her little piggies under the desk

we used to stay after school
to sneak around and smell her shoes
and this little piggy ran all the way home

what you learn in school today

bout how columbus
landed in cuba stuck a flag in the ground
how neil armstrong landed on the moon and stuck a flag in the ground
how rick rubin landed in rap and stuck a flag in the sound

hey you all look what I found

the east village
a human garden   a botanical class menagerie
with its own avant-garde beatnik color guard

that when asked to
present the colors of their flag

> *they go*   *white and ummm*
>   *bob kaufmann aaaand lets see uhhhh*
>   *oh yeah the angry guy*

hey leroi

i joined this peoples army
to seek that quintessential beat freedom
that only white boys seem to achieve

the rest of us
still dream about being so casual
being able to act up
with that bill murray i dont give a fuck   boom shaka laka
        boom shaka laka
        chief house rocker attitude

hey dude care to smoke a bowl   no regrets hold your breath
dont smoke buddha
cant stand sess
its takes two to make-ah thing go right

so i force a discourse
   wid corporal gregory corso
   his pissed on disciples fix bayonets
   point their self righteous rifles   at my writing

dont get upset but

> why dont you [blacks and other oppressed etc.]
> write more universally

does that mean write more white
drink tea in the morning
write about flowers n lust and poeticize the dust in the light rays

        dont pull my daisy

but like paul revere said
at end of his midnight ride   whoa

it never ceases to amaze me
that whenever these jazz crazed
               surly black berets
               police the proud grounds
               of their past
        they always
mention diane diprima last

            boom shaka laka
            boom shaka laka
            thats the fact jack

       i've heard   elvis donny hathaway
        and roberta flack rap about the ghetto
but in the village
       i can peruse stacks n stacks
       of used and overdue library books

rows n rows
           of mad magazine paperbacks
like Al Jaffee's   Snappy Answers
           to Stupid Questions

How does it feel to read in front of so many white people?

snappy answer #1: the tompkins sq. park zoo closes at 1:00am
snappy answer #2: *i feel the earth move under my feet*
                       i feel the sky tumblin down
snappy answer #3: sometimes i feel like othello in the last act
                    desdemona is thru
                    and now usin modern medieval seppuku
                    heez fixin to spill his noble guts to the public

    Soft you; a word or two before you go.
    I have done the state some service and they know't;
    . . . Speak of me as I am: nothing extenuate, . . .
    you must speak
    Of one that loved not wisely, but too well; . . .   340
    I took —by th'throat the . . . dog
    And smote him thus.   350

why you stabbeded my brother in the back
i be got no weapon

doin the hollywood shuffle
here in alphabet city
where the contradictions are so deep
you got
                         white supremacists
                         datin *black chicks*

where the tattooed unclenched fists of anarchists
talk bout if they had money
theyd start the revolution

when if theyd redeem
all the pop bottles

> they toss at the cops
> they could at least leaflet
> all the way to avenue D

but paulo friere multiculturalism and foucault
and the highbrow *whats wrong with the world*
handbilled and postered so and so
dont go into the projects

cuz thats where the for real
dispossessed pink slipped guerrillas in the mist stay at
hangin around   brass monkeys on the buzzards back

and in the middle of my rant
the man said
lighten up jack
straighten up and fly right
cool out and add a white boy to your jazz collection

so i attached gerry mulligans
hook n ladder long-ass sax
fire engine red hair to my wake up solo
this mornin i feel like
a black sideman playin poetic trumpet

> *my my aint that sumpthin*

a literary bojangles
inna military band
playin taps
> red black n greens at half-mast
> his bitterness iz dead

while uptowns fife n thumb drum corps
separates the trapezoids from the squares
      the raw from the done

         i polish up my buttons n buckles

         check out my reflection

         fakin the funk

         im ready for inspection
lace up my doc martens
and im marchin

hut-hop hop hop het-who
hut-hop hep who
lookin' good   lookin' good
      lookin' good like you should

DIANE DI PRIMA

Diane Di Prima, the mother of five children and the author of over thirty-five collections of prose and poetry, was born in Brooklyn in 1934 of first generation Italian-American parents. She dropped out of college after one year in 1951 and moved to the lower east side of Manhattan to write poetry and study. It was there she began a correspondence with Ezra Pound. Her cold-water flat became a haven for dancers, musicians, poets, and painters. Alan Ginsberg and Jack Kerouac passed through there on the way to Morocco. One of the major figures of the beat movement, she is the author of the classic *Memoir of a Beatnik*, and coeditor with Amiri Baraka of the literary newsletter *The Floating Bear*, for which she was arrested by the FBI for obscenity. She also took part in Timothy Leary's psychedelic community at Millbrook in upstate New York. For the last thirty years she has lived and worked in northern California. She says she found a vast permission in the jazz she heard and the abstract expressionist paintings she saw in New York in the 50s and 60s. The poem for her became an improvised graph following the movements of emotion. The poem for Di Prima is a place to contain oppositions and contradictions, a revolutionary endeavor that reawakens the imagination, without which she believes life is not worth living. She believes there is a worldwide war going on against the imagination, and that we have to resist at all costs the flattening and deadening of our dreams. "April Fool Birthday Poem for Grandpa" is written for her maternal grandfather, Dominic Mallozzi, an active anarchist and associate of Emma Goldman. The poem "Ode to Elegance" praises the exactness of the math equation, the grace of human life, and how every particular thing does what it does with spare perfection.

APRIL FOOL BIRTHDAY POEM
FOR GRANDPA

Today is your
birthday and I have tried
writing these things before,
but now
in the gathering madness, I want to
thank you
for telling me what to expect
for pulling
no punches, back there in that scrubbed Bronx parlor
thank you
for honestly weeping in time to
innumerable heartbreaking
italian operas for
pulling my hair when I
pulled the leaves off the trees so I'd
know how it feels, we are
involved in it now, revolution, up to our
knees and the tide is rising, I embrace
strangers on the street, filled with their love and
mine, the love you told us had to come or we
die, told them all in that Bronx park, me listening in
spring Bronx dusk, breathing stars, so glorious
to me your white hair, your height your fierce
blue eyes, rare among italians, I stood
a ways off, looking up at you, my grandpa
people listened to, I stand
a ways off listening as I pour out soup
young men with light in their faces
at my table, talking love, talking revolution
which is love, spelled backwards, how
you would love us all, would thunder your anarchist wisdom

at us, would thunder Dante, and Giordano Bruno, orderly men
bent to your ends, well I want you to know
we do it for you, and your ilk, for Carlo Tresca,
for Sacco and Vanzetti, without knowing
it, or thinking about it, as we do it for Aubrey Beardsley
Oscar Wilde (all street lights
shall be purple), do it
for Trotsky and Shelley and big/dumb
Kropotkin
Eisenstein's Strike people, Jean Cocteau's ennui, we do it for
the stars over the Bronx
that they may look on earth
and not be ashamed.

ODE TO ELEGANCE

AND PRAISE THE GRACE, the elegance of body. Your hands,
flesh of my children, thin giraffes
raising themselves in the sun on distant plains
The elegance of mantis and of beetle
The clear precisions of the shooting stars
colors of water
sounds on the city air
directio voluntatis, the clear will
shining like rubies through the lucid eyes
"the city of Dioce"
long eyes of cats in the grass

the slender elegance of scorpions
lovers of death
flash of the hunting knife

the thin high noise in the air
the breath of Kali
precision of the fingernail on flesh
pastels of Beardsley
pain of a century

that the skin should lie so elegantly on the air
that the black night should penetrate so gently
that treason should shine like stars
the clarity
of dawn, of murder, of the running tide

the subtle stuff of slime, the river mosses
with light inwoven
the elegance of the skull
the phosphorescence of the ending body
exposed to earth to air water or fire
will o'the wisp, a marsh light, star to star
the holy mother of the cremation ground

let us now praise all fleshly consummations
(the elegance of sweat)
initiation
into the burning loneliness of this place
desert of salt
immense intoxication
in this white light
under this rush of wind
all things teem forth like dust motes in the air

that all things send forth love, inanimate
that all these loves have mingled in the air
and set up a great clangor

in the nodes
heart of this sound, this deadly spirit love
a cosmos comes to birth

let the pure pain tear your throat till you spit blood
cry out! rejoice!
that which must come to birth
even the goddessmother cannot dream of

we climb from rung to rung, a circular
undeviating golden, perfect ladder
of ages, long forgotten, to be told
over and over, like a string of prayerbeads

"the ferris wheel has started up again"

LORNA DEE CERVANTES

Chicana poet Lorna Dee Cervantes grew up in the horseshoe bar-
rio of San Jose, California. She currently lives and teaches in Col-
orado. She says she wrote her poems in secret, under the shadow of
the freeway. In the 70s she became involved with a Chicano theater
group. After graduation, she traveled with them to Mexico, and in
front of hundreds of people she learned that poetry and politics
could merge. The theater group was just as invested in enacting
social change as in making art. Cervantes believes that poetry saves
lives. While it can't really put food on the table, she believes it is
food for the soul, often giving the spiritual nourishment and impe-
tus we need to act. She says she writes "docupoetry," where poetic,
symbolic, and personal truths interweave with historical fact; her
work expands our notion of what history and poetry can be. For
example, in the following poem, the banana is compared to a beau-
tiful flower, but she also calls them "gold claws" as she describes the
graves of the campesinos who were murdered during a strike on a
banana plantation. "Bananas" was generated from a letter that Cer-
vantes received from a theoretical physicist in Estonia who saw par-
allels between the struggle of Mexican-Americans in this country
and what was going on in Estonia. Cervantes' imagination was
sparked by the fact that a physicist had to prove the existence of
bananas to his children. This feature was postponed for several
months because of news stories on the bombing of Iraq in 1999.

BANANAS
for Indrek

I

In Estonia, Indrek is taking his children
to the Dollar Market to look at bananas.
He wants them to know about the presence of fruit,
about globes of light tart to the tongue, about the
twang of tangelos, the cloth of persimmons,
the dull little mons of kiwi. There is not a chance
for a taste. Where rubles are scarce, dollars are harder.
Even beef is doled out welfare-thin on Saturday's platter.
They light the few candles not reserved for the dead,
and try not to think of small bites in the coming winter,
of irradiated fields or the diminished catch in the fisherman's
net. They tell of bananas yellow as daffodils. And mango—
which tastes as if the whole world came out from her womb.

II

Colombia, 1928, bananas rot in the fields.
A strip of lost villages between railyard
and cemetery. The United Fruit Company train,
a yellow painted slug, eats up the swamps and jungle.
Campesinos replace Indians who are a dream
and a rubble of bloody stones hacked into coffins:
malaria, tuberculosis, cholera, machetes of the jefes.
They become like the empty carts that shatter
the landscape. Their hands, no longer pulling the teats
from the trees, now twist into death, into silence
and obedience. They wait in Aracataca, poised as
statues between hemispheres. They would rather be
tilling the plots for black beans. They would rather grow
wings and rise as pericos—parrots, poets, clowns, a word
which means all this and whose task is messenger

from Mítla, the underworld, where the ancestors
of the slain arise with the vengeance of Tláloc. A stench
permeates the wind as bananas, black on the stumps, char
into odor. The murdered Mestizos have long been cleared
and begin their new duties as fertilizer for the plantations.
Feathers fall over the newly spaded soil: turquoise,
scarlet, azure, quetzál, and yellow litters
the graves like gold claws of bananas.

III

Dear I,
The 3'x6' boxes in front of the hippie
market in Boulder are radiant with marigolds, some
with heads big as my Indian face. They signify
death to me, as it is Labor Day and already
I am making up the guest list for my Día de los Muertos
altar. I'll need maravillas so this year I plant caléndulas
for blooming through snow that will fall before November.
I am shopping for "no-spray" bananas. I forego
the Dole and Chiquita, that name that always made me
blush for being christened with that title. But now
I am only a little small, though still brown enough
for the—Where are you from? Probably my ancestors
planted a placenta here as well as on my Califas coast
where alien shellfish replaced native mussels,
clams and oysters in 1886. I'm from the 21st Century,
I tell them, and feel rude for it—when all I desire
is bananas without pesticides. They're smaller
than plantains which are green outside and firm
and golden when sliced. Fried in butter
they turn yellow as over-ripe fruit. And sweet.
I ask the produce manager how to crate and
pack bananas to Estonia. She glares at me
suspiciously: You can't do that. I know.

There must be some law. You might spread
diseases. They would arrive as mush, anyway.
I am thinking of children in Estonia with
no fried plátanos to eat with their fish as
the Blond turns away, still without shedding
a smile at me, Hija del Sol, Earth's Daughter, lover
of bananas. I buy up Baltic wheat. I buy up organic
bananas, butter y canéla. I ship banana bread.

IV

At Big Mountain uranium
sings through the dreams of the people.
Women dress in glowing symmetries, sheep
clouds gather below the bluffs, sundown
sandstone blooms in four corners. Smell of sage
penetrates as state tractors with chains trawl the resistant
plants, gouging anew the tribal borders, uprooting
all in their path like Amazonian ants, breaking
the hearts of the widows. Elders and children
cut the fence again and again as wind whips
the waist of ancient rock. Sheep nip across
centuries in the people's blood, and are carried
off by the Federal choppers waiting in the canyon
with orders and slings. A long winter, little wool
to spin, medicine lost in the desecration of the desert.
Old women weep as the camera rolls on the dark
side of conquest. Encounter rerun. Uranium. 1992.

V

I worry about winter in a place
I've never been, about exiles in their
homeland gathered around a fire,
about the slavery of substance and
gruel: Will there be enough to eat?

Will there be enough to feed? And
they dream of beaches and pies, hemispheres
of soft fruit found only in the heat of the planet.
Sugar canes, like Geiger counters, seek out tropics;
and dictate a Resolution to stun the tongues of those
who can afford to pay: imported plums, bullets,
black caviar large as peas, smoked meats
the color of Southern lynchings, what we don't
discuss in letters.
You are out of work.
Not many jobs today for high physicists
in Estonia, you say. Poetry, though, is food
for the soul. And bread? What is cake before
corn and the potato? Before the encounter
of animals, women and wheat? Stocks high
these days in survival products, 500 years later tomato
size tumors bloom in the necks of the pickers.
On my coast, Diablo dominates the golden hills,
the faultlines. On ancestral land Vandenberg shoots nuclear
payloads to Kwajalein, a Pacific atoll, where 68% of all
infants are born amphibian or anemones. But poetry
is for the soul. I speak of spirit, the yellow seed
in air as life is the seed in water, and the poetry
of Improbability, the magic in the Movement
of quarks and sunlight, the subtle basketry
of hadrons and neutrinos of color, how what you do
is what you get—bananas or worry.
What do you say? Your friend,
a Chicana poet.

PAUL MULDOON

Much of Paul Muldoon's work recalls the life and history of rural county Armagh in Northern Ireland where he grew up. His father was a farmer who raised cauliflower and mushrooms; his mother was a teacher. Many of his poems explore history and the complexity of human emotions. He says there are very few poems about the conditions of joy in the world. "The Birth," a poem about the birth of his daughter, becomes a miraculous container, packed with stuff, as he tries to order, name, or "staple" in feelings of inexpressible joy. In the middle of the poem is a hidden alphabet of the world's linguistic and material wonders. The fourteen lines of "The Briefcase" open and close (like a briefcase) on a hinge made of symmetrical rhymes. The poem is a negotiation between two kingdoms: the commonplace, the clichéd—"the raging torrents," the "open sea"—and what lies beyond that common place, exploring those two kingdoms, and in doing so perhaps moving beyond the limitations of the material self. An ordinary bus token is compared to an obol, a little coin that in ancient times was placed in the mouth of the dead. In this way, the ordinary becomes extraordinary and luminous, offering mystical possibilities for travel.

THE BIRTH

Seven o'clock. The seventh day of the seventh month of the year.
No sooner have I got myself up in lime-green scrubs,
a sterile cap and mask,
and taken my place at the head of the table

than the windlass-women ply their shears
and gralloch-grub
for a footling foot, then, warming to their task,
haul into the inestimable

realm of apple-blossoms and chanterelles and damsons and eel-spears
and foxes and the general hubbub
of inkies and jennets and Kickapoos with their lemniscs
or peekaboo-quiffs of Russian sable

and tallow-unctuous vernix, into the realm of the widgeon
the 'whew' or 'yellow-poll', not the 'zuizin'

Dorothy Aoife Korelitz Muldoon: I watch through floods of tears
as they give her a quick rub-a-dub
and whisk
her off to the nursery, then check their staple-guns for staples.

ANSEO

When the Master was calling the roll
At the primary school in Collegelands,
You were meant to call back *Anseo*
And raise your hand
As your name occurred.

Anseo, meaning here, here and now,
All present and correct,
Was the first word of Irish I spoke.
The last name on the ledger
Belonged to Joseph Mary Plunkett Ward
And was followed, as often as not,
By silence, knowing looks,
A nod and a wink, the Master's droll
'And where's our little Ward-of-court?'

I remember the first time he came back
The Master had sent him out
Along the hedges
To weigh up for himself and cut
A stick with which he would be beaten.
After a while, nothing was spoken;
He would arrive as a matter of course
With an ash-plant, a salley-rod.
Or, finally, the hazel-wand
He had whittled down to a whip-lash,
Its twist of red and yellow lacquers
Sanded and polished,
And altogether so delicately wrought
That he had engraved his initials on it.

I last met Joseph Mary Plunkett Ward
In a pub just over the Irish border.
He was living in the open,
In a secret camp
On the other side of the mountain.
He was fighting for Ireland,
Making things happen.
And he told me, Joe Ward,
Of how he had risen through the ranks

To Quartermaster, Commandant:
How every morning at parade
His volunteers would call back *Anseo*
And raise their hands
As their names occurred.

THE BRIEFCASE
for Seamus Heaney

I held the briefcase at arm's length from me;
the oxblood or liver
eelskin with which it was covered
had suddenly grown supple.

I'd been waiting in line for the cross-town
bus when an almighty cloudburst
left the sidewalk a raging torrent.

And though it contained only the first
inkling of this poem, I knew I daren't
set the briefcase down
to slap my pockets for an obol—

for fear it might slink into a culvert
and strike out along the East River
for the sea. By which I mean the 'open' sea.

LUCILLE CLIFTON

When Lucille Clifton's first book of poems was published in 1969, her children were 7, 5, 4, 3, 2, and 1. Between chasing toddlers and changing diapers, she says she learned to hold a poem inside her head until she had time to get it down on paper. And now, a quarter of a century later, she is a college professor with enough collections of prose, children's books, and poetry to fill a bookshelf. She says she still likes to write in the middle of things, that she needs the sounds of the world going on around her, human noise, to create that most human of activities—poetry. Clifton believes that a poem is an act of remembering and that forgetting is a perilous activity in a culture that embraces an "endless present." In poetry she hopes to conjure history and name her inheritances, which she says are beauty, power, magic, and most importantly the oddness in us. Many of her poems deal with the ways families and communities can empower and nurture children and also harm them. She wants to capture the world "whole"—to work with the contradictions of life in a straight-forward style that is accessible and emotionally complex.

s a m

if he could have kept
the sky in his dark hand
he would have pulled it down
and held it.
it would have called him lord
as did the skinny women
in virginia. if he
could have gone to school
he would have learned to write
his story and not live it.
if he could have done better
he would have. oh stars
and stripes forever,
what did you do to my father?

j u n e 20

i will be born in one week
to a frowned forehead of a woman
and a man whose fingers will itch
to enter me. she will crochet
a dress for me of silver
and he will carry me in it.
they will do for each other
all that they can
but it will not be enough.
none of us know that we will not
smile again for years,
that she will not live long.
in one week i will emerge face first
into their temporary joy.

homage to my hips

these hips are big hips
they need space to
move around in.
they don't fit into little
petty places. these hips
are free hips.
they don't like to be held back.
these hips have never been enslaved,
they go where they want to go
they do what they want to do.
these hips are mighty hips.
these hips are magic hips.
i have known them
to put a spell on a man and
spin him like a top!

daughters

woman who shines at the head
of my grandmother's bed,
brilliant woman, i like to think
you whispered into her ear
instructions. i like to think
you are the oddness in us,
you are the arrow
that pierced our plain skin
and made us fancy women;
my wild witch gran, my magic mama,
and even these gaudy girls.
i like to think you gave us

extraordinary power and to
protect us, you became the name
we were cautioned to forget.
it is enough,
you must have murmured,
to remember that i was
and that you are. woman, i am
lucille, which stands for light,
daughter of thelma, daughter
of georgia, daughter of
dazzling you.

NAOMI SHIHAB NYE

Naomi Shihab Nye makes her home near the Alamo in San Antonio, Texas, and like the Alamo she is a local treasure—one day giving a talk to the Officers' Wives Club, the next working with third graders on a poetry writing lesson. This Palestinian-American poet said she learned to write poetry by taking in the rich sensory experiences of her childhood—the sugary bite of the mint snowball her great-grandfather served at his small town drugstore, the aromas of orange blossoms and olive oil soap from her uncle's house on the West Bank, the songs and stories she overheard at the dinner table in her home in St. Louis where her parents welcomed and fed poets, scholars, and travelers from all over the world. We often wait for some splendid experience to overtake and transform us forever, but Nye's poems find that the most transformative experiences are to be found in small, seemingly insignificant things: these are the true splendid moments. In one poem, she commemorates the wondrous and juicy Stonewall peaches of the Texas Hill Country. She says, "tangible small objects are what I live for and am attracted to. Since I was a child, I have felt that little inanimate things were very wise, that they had their own wisdom, something to teach me if I could only pay the right kind of attention to them." She was influenced by her Palestinian grandmother who lived to be 106 years old and once said, "one moment on top of the earth is better than a thousand moments under the earth."

MY FRIEND'S DIVORCE

I want her
to dig up
every plant
in her garden
the pansies
the pentas
roses
ranunculus
thyme and lilies
the thing nobody knows
the name of
unwind the morning glories
from the wire windows
of the fence
take the blooming
and the almost-blooming
and the dormant
especially the dormant
and then
and then
plant them in her new yard
on the other side
of town
and see how
they breathe

GOING FOR PEACHES,
FREDERICKSBURG, TEXAS

Those with experience look for a special kind.
Red Globe, the skin slips off like a fine silk camisole.
Boy breaks one open with his hands. Yes, it's good,
my old relatives say, but we'll look around.
They want me to stop at every peach stand
between Stonewall and Fredericksburg,
leave the air conditioner running,
jump out and ask the price.

Coming up here they talked about
the best ways to die. One favors a plane crash,
but not over a city. One wants to make sure
her grass is watered when she goes.
Ladies, ladies! This peach is fine,
it blushes on both sides.
But they want to keep driving.

In Fredericksburg the houses are stone,
they remind me of wristwatches, glass polished,
years ticking by in each wall.
I don't like stone, says one. What if it fell?
I don't like Fredericksburg, says the other.
Too many Germans driving too slow.
She herself is German as Stuttgart.
The day presses forward wearing complaints,
charms on its bony wrist.

Actually ladies, (I can't resist),
I don't think you wanted peaches after all,
you just wanted a nip of scenery,

some hills to tuck behind your heads.
The buying starts immediately, from a scarfed woman
who says she gave up teachin' for peachin'.
She has us sign a guest book.
One aunt insists on reloading into her box
to see the fruit on the bottom.
One rejects any slight bruise.
But Ma'am, the seller insists, nature isn't perfect.
Her hands are spotted, like a peach.

On the road, cars weave loose patterns between lanes.
We will float in flowery peach-smell
back to our separate kettles, our private tables
and knives, and line up the bounty,
deciding which ones go where.
A canned peach, says one aunt, lasts ten years.
She was 87 last week. But a frozen peach
tastes better on ice cream.
Everything we have learned so far,
skins alive and ripening, on a day
that was real to us, that was summer,
motion going out and memory coming in.

WEDDING CAKE

Once on a plane
a woman asked me to hold her baby
and disappeared.
I figured it was safe,
our being on a plane and all.
How far could she go?

She returned one hour later,
having changed her clothes
and washed her hair.
I didn't recognize her.

By this time the baby
and I had examined
each other's necks.
We had cried a little.
I had a silver bracelet
and a watch.
Gold studs glittered
in the baby's ears.
She wore a tiny white dress
leafed with layers
like a wedding cake.

I did not want
to give her back.

The baby's curls coiled tightly
against her scalp,
another alphabet.
I read *new new new.*
My mother gets tired.
I'll chew your hand.
The baby left my skirt crumpled,
my lap aching.
Now I'm her secret guardian,
the little nub of dream
that rises slightly
but won't come clear.

As she grows,
as she feels ill at ease,
I'll bob my knee.

What will she forget?
Whom will she marry?
He'd better check with me.
I'll say once she flew
dressed like a cake
between two doilies of cloud.
She could slip the card into a pocket,
pull it out.
Already she knew the small finger
was funnier than the whole arm.

RICHARD BLANCO

Cuban-American poet Richard Blanco says he was invented in Cuba, assembled in Spain, and imported to the United States. His parents fled Cuba for Spain in 1968, and then came to the U.S. where they named their new son after the newly elected President Richard Nixon. For many years, Blanco made his living as a civil engineer, building bridges and studying water systems in south Florida. Blanco's ambivalence about cultural assimilation and anger at a lost past are powerfully rendered through lush, wistful lyrics and exacting imagery. The lines have a rocking, lilting feel of someone who has grown up near the ocean. The Décima Guajira is a Cuban poetic form, often improvised to music at parties after a few belts of rum.

DÉCIMA GUAJIRA

I

> *Veo la tierra amada*
> *que marcó mis padres pasos*
> *dentro estos muertos ojos*
> *ahora baila y canta*
> *el azúcar, la décima.*

The *guajiro* arias of *la décima* drift
in the lifted dust of brackish shadows
over dancing sugar cane that follows
the meter, the rhyme, the ten line craft
of my grandfather's melancholy gift.

II

> *Bajo tu manta de polvo*
> *aquí encuentro y guardo*
> *mi alma tallada en mármol*
> *como un talismán de caracol*
> *que guardo en la mano.*

It is this mantle of dust that keeps
the marble music, the drifting sand
of footprints blown over this loved land;
the talismans in the hands of my sleep
that sing so slow and so very deep.

PHOTO SHOP

These faces are fifteen under faux diamond tiaras
and grandmother's smuggled *brillantes;*
these faces are pierced with the mango smiles
that dress hopeful *Teresitas* and *Marías*—
quinceañeras with coffee bean eyes;
these pearl faces are mother's taffeta dream,
a decorated anguish in painful pink manicures.
These young faces can't remember that last day—
the innocence of their small steps into the propeller
plane drifting above palms waving elegant farewells.
These barefoot faces are those red mountains
never climbed, a Caribbean never drunk,
they are a *guajiro* sugar never tasted.
These faces are displaced *Miritas* and *Susanitas.*
These faces are a 50's revolution
they are the Beatles and battles,
they are Celia Cruz—AZUCAR—loud and brown;
these faces rock-n-roll and roll their r's,
they are eery *botánicas* and Seven-Elevens.
These fiery faces are rifles and bongos,
they are *maracas* shaking, *machetes* hacking;
these faces carry too many names:
their white eyes are toppling dominos
their glossy eyes are rum and iced tea
their African eyes are gods and Castilian saints
haloed with the finest *tabaco* smoke.
These faces rest an entire ocean on Taino eyebrows;
they are Kennedy, Batista and Nixon,
they are a dragon in uniform;
these faces are singing two anthems,
nailed against walls, the walls are chipping.

These overflowing faces are swollen barrels
with rusting hoops and corset seams straining;
these faces are beans: black, red, white and blue,
with steaming rice on chipped china;
these faces are pork fat and lace gowns.
These standing faces are a sentinel —
when the Vietnamese kitchen next door stops
when the alley veils itself and closes like a fresh widow
when the flower shop draws in buckets of red carnations
when gold and diamonds are pulled from late windows
when neon flashes relieve the sun over these fading faces.
These chromatic faces are nothing important,
they are *nada* we need to understand,
they will transform in their photo chemistry,
these faces will collage very Americanly.

THE SILVER SANDS

Before the revival of quartz pinks and icy blues
on this neon beach of Art Deco hotels and boutiques,
there were the twilight verandas lined with retirees,
the cataract eyes of Mrs. Stein who would take us
for mezzanine bingo and pancakes at Wolfies;
I remember her beautiful orthopedic wobble.

Before sequined starlets popping out of limousine doors
and booze on the breath of every glitter-paved street,
there were the five-year-old summers of flamingo towels,
transistor radios blaring something in Spanish we ignored,
only curious of driftwood, washed-up starfish and jellyfish,
the beauty of broken conchs and our moated sand castles.

Before the widened sidewalks and pretentious *cafés*
where I take my cappuccino sprinkled with cinnamon,
our mothers were peacocks in flowered bathing caps
posing for sandy Polaroids like pageant contestants;
there were fifteen-cent Cokes to their ruby lips
and there was nothing their beauty couldn't conquer.

Before the demolition of the Silver Sands Hotel,
our fathers spun dominos under the thatch-palm gazebos,
drank then insulted the scenery: *Nada like our Varadero,*
there the sand was powder; the water truly aquamarine.
I remember the poor magic of those voices—
how beautifully they remembered beauty.

ALBERT GOLDBARTH

Rollicking, manic forays, Albert Goldbarth's poems take off at otherworldly speed, fueled by supermarket tabloids glancing off real life and his own experiences—whether that's taking a TV dramatist's view of a murder or meditating on the disappearance of a child whose picture is on the side of a milk carton. He refuses to touch a computer, instead writing all of his poems with a pen in a spiral notebook. Though he rejects technology in this area of his life, his poems are packed with techno-speech and contemporary jargon. In "Coinages: A Fairy Tale," Goldbarth spins together and yokes a multitiude of disparate images, vocabularies, and associations in an attempt to narrow the space between the words on the page, and the real objects, lives, and experiences they signify. His poems are takes, re-takes, and double-takes on the strange and mysterious conjunctions involved in our cosmic, historical, and personal lives. A sense of history is indispensable to his poetry.

COINAGES: A FAIRY TALE

On May 1, 1947, when *airlift* barely existed, my father
lay down beside my mother. He wasn't my father
yet, she wasn't my mother, not technically, the late sun
played the scales of light on the lake at Indian Lodge State Park,
and *rocket-booster* was new by a year, and *thruway*
only by two, and *sputnik* waited somewhere
in the clouded-over swales of the future and, beyond it,
pixel, rolfing, homeboy, floated
in a *cyberspace* too far-removed and conceptual
even to be defined by cloud. He stroked her. She stirred
in her veil of slumber—when was the last time
anyone "slumbered," except in a poem?—but didn't wake.
Not that he wanted to wake her: only to stay
in contact with this singular, corporeal thing they'd made
of themselves amid the chenille and gas heat of the room.
It would be night soon. It would be dusk, and then
the dreamy, let's say the oneiric, nighttime.
Macrobiotic would come into being, *fractal, rock-and-roll.*
The first reported use of *twofer, LP, fax* is 1948.
Spelunker, 1946, and *cybernetics, TV, vitamin B-12,* were
newfangled, still as if with the glister
of someone's original utterance on them. Others,
say, the *kit bag* that they'd lazily left open near the radio, as in
"pack up your troubles in your ol' kit bag and smile,
darn you, smile"—were even now
half-insubstantial, like a remnant
foxfire glimmering richly over a mound of verbal mulch.
Wingding, riffraff, tittle-tattle: holding even. I'm not saying
vocabulary is people, or anything easily
equational like that—although surely
we've all known a generation going *naught* and *o'er* and *nary*
that disappeared with its language. How

was the pulse of *boogie-woogie* doing? *demesne? lapsarian?*
He looked out the window—as solid by now with darkness
as a tile trivet. Obsidian. Impenetrable.
He looked *at* it—or *through* it—or looked crystal ball-like *into* it
at himself, and tried to practice things he'd been wanting to say.
Outside, in an invisible ripple, *eleemosynary* faded
further from the fundament of human use—and *farrier*
and *haberdasher* and *lyre* and *tocsin* and *arras* and *yore*.
When was the last time a liar dissembled, the cressets were lit,
the nefarious were vilified? My father said "Albert"
—that was the name they'd decided on, for a boy. He breathed it
into the night, into the turning invisible
bingo drum of give-and-take out there, where *radar* was new
and dynastic, and *transistor* was equally sturdy,
and *aerosporin*, and the brave new world of *xerox* and *laser* and *virtual reality*
held initiating breath in abeyance, somewhere
yonder in future time. "Albert"—it had been his father's name.
My mother opened her eyes now, she was sprawled in a daringly brief,
but sensibly flannel, nightie—exactly
under the ceiling fan, that turned like the oars of rowers
who keep circling over some fabulous discovery below.
That's what my father thought: it was fabulous! *They*
were fabulous! And he was terrified,
too; he knew that over the dark hills in the dark night,
varlets waited, and scurrilous knaves, and goons and racketeers,
he knew the darkness spewed forth villainy and predation the way
a spoiled cheese frothed maggots—after all,
he'd searched out bodies in the coal mine
with a thin wood lathe they'd issued him for feeling through
the seepage, and he'd lounged around the poolrooms
where the ward boss and his thick, pomaded cronies
held their shabby court. By this, and by the other signs
a body ages into itself, he understood the emptiness
in everything, he understood it long before

neutrino and *pulsar* and *chaos theory* would be
the current buzz, and simply standing there
in his half-price Florsheim wingtip brogues he'd polished
to an onyx shine, he understood a man and a woman
clatter for the casual amusement of the gods
like pea gravel flung in an oil drum. All this,
and a sense of grandiosity, of flame and aching sweetness
in the coils of him, and of the Milky Way he'd touched increasingly
alive in her skin . . . all this, and more, was asking him, now,
to be brought into speech, on May 1, 1947,
at Indian Lodge State Park. He swallowed,
and was silent, and shook, until she saw
and asked what was the matter.
He didn't have the words.

HOW EASY IT IS

A family is murdered: husband, wife,
a 5- and 6-year-old. The bolt is sawed off
cleanly, and the slits in the throats
are neat professional slits,
as if four envelopes were opened: even the signature
the killer left, a scoring on the cheek of each,
is neatly figured, bingo- or tictactoe-like.
The town is horrified. Although these deaths
are dust motes in the dunes of death
that pile and reshape themselves and could cover a city
daily—still, the town in which these four
were slaughtered is horrified, and that night
wives and husbands surreptitiously eye
the common comings and goings of their own homes
with emotions that surpasseth understanding.

There are few clues. Days go by. A man
admits to having nightmares, and is sure
he committed the murders while in a trance,
and shows up weeping at the station. A woman
phones, all week she hasn't been able to bring herself
to lift the kitchen knife to simply dice a carrot,
even her emery file makes her skin crawl: she did it,
she knows she did it, sleepwalking, hypnotized,
let them come and drag her to a cell.
The detective assigned to the case wakes up
that day, and dons his good detectiveware, and
kisses his wife and son on their cheeks,
and drives to an office he finds is swimming
in various written, phoned, and in-person confessions.
They come from every neighboring state. It seems
that half the planet realizes how easy it is
to damage a family. There are hundreds of confessions
and not one real suspect. Maybe the local
cops aren't doing a good enough job. A pressure
fills the squad room. There are forms, and reporters,
and more forms, and a nasty call from the mayor,
and by day's end our detective is a tightening engine
of knots being powered by coffee. How did it
go, his wife asks; GODDAMMIT, he says,
in front of the son,
in the loudest voice he's used in their own
six years together. She brings her hands up
to the sides of her face, as if he's actually hurt her there.

AN EXPLANATION

They say this really happened, in the Church of Eternal Light:
a penitent dropped to the floor wearing nothing but sweat, she
spasmed like some snake on an electrified wire, she uttered
angel eldestspeech, and then she disappeared—they mean
totally, and at once. First the entire tarpaper room gave a shudder,
and then she disappeared—at once, and totally.
Nobody understands it. Well,
maybe I understand it. Once, in 8th grade, Denton Nashbell
had an epileptic seizure. Mrs. Modderhock squatted
above where he flapped like something half a person
half a pennant, she was pressing a filthy spoon to his tongue.
I've remembered him 25 years now. And—that woman? she
was the universe's tongue the universe
swallowed. That's as good an explanation as any.
Once, in sleep, you started a dream soliloquy,
the grammar of which is snow on fire, the words are
neuron-scrawl, are words the elements sing to their molecules . . .
—I threw myself across you.
It wasn't sex this time. I just wanted to keep you
beside me, in this world.

CARRIE ALLEN McCRAY

It wasn't until Carrie Allen McCray was seventy-three that she found her true calling as a poet. Now almost ninety, she has made up for lost time—she's written an award-winning collection of poems, a memoir, and a novel. In her prose and poetry she writes about her family's history: about her grandmother's forbidden relationship with a confederate general; the Harlem Renaissance writers who visited her home as a child; and a long poem about Ota Benga, an African pygmy tribesman who was brought by missionaries to the United States from the Belgian Congo and displayed in a cage at the Bronx Zoo. He later lived with McCray's family when she was growing up. McCray shows how poetry is an alternative medium for documenting the past, presenting us with experiences and events that are usually left out of the news or history books. Her poems are a living repository of American history, an alternative kind of telling, as she connects, with great clarity and directness, the personal particular experiences of her life to larger historical and social events.

THOUGHTS AT THE GRAVE SITE

October 1935

All I could see
was you in your
red felt hat
walking briskly
out the front door
on the way to
the "fight"
you, who integrated
the living in our
small town
being lowered now
into a segregated
corner of the
graveyard

*To my mother, longtime fighter
for equality and justice*

STRANGE PATTERNS

When I was a young child
in Lynchburg, Virginia
I could not ride the
trolley car sitting next
to our white neighbor
But could sit, nestled
close to her
under her grape arbor

swinging my feet
eating her scuppernongs
and drinking tall, cold
glasses of lemonade
she offered us on
hot, dry summer days

When I was a young child
moving to Montclair, New Jersey
I could now ride the
trolley car sitting next
to our white neighbor
but did not dare
cross the bitter line
that separated our house
from hers
and she never offered us
tall, cold glasses of lemonade
on hot, dry summer days

TWO WAYS TO COOK MACARONI AND CHEESE FOR PASTOR

The high-pitched Soprano
    over horn-rimmed glasses
looks at robust Contralto,
    "Hmm, that the way you make
macaroni and cheese for Pastor?"

"Yeah," Contralto deep-voices,
    "That's the way I makes
macaroni and cheese for Pastor."

"Well, Pastor loves mine," Soprano
     chirps, "cause it's so full
of cheese, cheese oozing all
     over the top, runnin' all
down the side," her voice
     seductive.

"Well, Pastor loves mine,"
     Contralto's voice deepens,
"cause it's big and round
     and full of all kinds of
good things.

"I boils that macaroni,
     puts heavy cream, lots of
cheese, milk, eggs, butter,
     and Pastor, he always say,
'Um-um, Miz Lizzie, yo'
     macaroni and cheese
the best I ever had.'"

Soprano turns up her nose
     and in an accusatory tone
admonishes Contralto,
     "I don' put heavy cream
in mine. You know Pastor
     has a bad heart.
You could kill Pastor?

"I put a little cre-e-e-m cheese
     in mine
And Pastor, he always say,
     'Um, um, Miz Sadie, yo'

macaroni and cheese
   the best I ever had.'"

TRADE OFF

What is this guilt
You're trying to heap
upon me like bales of
cotton
No, life did not take
me into the fields
beside you
But I would gladly
carry your bales,
if you could bear
my griefs

ANEMONE

For Molly Blackburn, lifelong fighter against apartheid

You could have spent
your time, as some,
among the wood anemone
or playing bridge on
afternoons with ladies fancy.

Instead you chose
the brambled path
where walked the
darker brother.

BELLE WARING

Belle Waring grew up in Virginia. Her grandfather, a country doctor who made house calls and knew all his patients' names and stories, had a big influence on her. She decided she wanted to be a doctor just like him and so became a nurse as a way to put herself through medical school. While there she quickly realized that her grandfather's kind of practice did not exist anymore in America, so she became a poet instead. Many of her poems come out of the world of nursing, healing, and hospitals. She says working as an intensive care nurse for over seventeen years taught her about making a poem. The detailed records and notes nurses keep at the end of each shift required her to be thorough, concise, and disciplined. With klieg light directness, Waring's poems deliver us into the world of operating rooms and birthing tables. Some poems are written out of an urgent desire to bear witness to the world, to name the unspeakable and horrific. The poem is an act of unsilencing, both confession and testimony. In "It Was My First Nursing Job" she repeats the word "witness" several times and each time it resonates in a different way. Waring says the poem is not so much about a sadistic doctor as it is simply a plea, a poem that humbly begs pardon. She said part of nursing and part of poetry is about picking up the pieces. "So Get Over It, Honey" is a remedy, made from a tonic of humor, stamina, and faith in the magic of the world's earthly delights.

IT WAS MY FIRST NURSING JOB

and I was stupid in it. I thought a doctor would not be unkind.
One wouldn't wait for a laboring woman to dilate to ten cm.

He'd brace one hand up his patient's vagina,
clamp the other on her pregnant belly, and force the fetus

through an eight-centimeter cervix.
She tore, of course. Bled.

Stellate lacerations extend from the cervix
like an asterisk. The staff nurses stormed and hissed

but the head nurse shrugged, *He doesn't like to wait around.*
No other doctor witnessed what he did. The man was an elder

in his church. He chattered and smiled broadly as he worked.
He wore the biggest gloves we could stock.

It was my first real job and I was scared in it.
One night a patient of his was admitted

bleeding. The charge nurse said, *He won't rip her.*
You take this one.

So I took her.
She quickly delivered a dead baby boy.

Not long dead—you could tell by the skin, intact.
But long enough.

When I wrapped him in a blanket, the doctor flipped open the cover
to let the mother view the body, according to custom.

The baby lay beside her.
He lay stretched out and still.

What a pity, the doctor said.
He seized the baby's penis between his own forefinger and thumb.

It was the first time I had ever seen a male not circumcised
and I was taken aback by the beauty of it.

Look, said the doctor, *A little boy. Just what we wanted.*
His hand, huge on the child, held the penis as if he'd found

a lovecharm hidden in his grandmother's linen.
And then he dropped it.

The mother didn't make a sound.
When the doctor left, she said to me in a far flat voice

I called and told him I was bleeding bad.
He told me not to worry.

I don't remember what I said. Just that
when I escorted her husband from the lobby

the doctor had already gone home. The new father followed me
with a joyful strut. I thought *Sweet Jesus Christ*

—*Did the doctor speak to you?*
—*No ma'am, the father said.*

I said quick-as-I-could-so-I-wouldn't-have-to-think—
The baby didn't make it.

The man doubled over. I told him all wrong.
I would do it all over again.

Say—
Please, sir. Sit down. I'm so very sorry to tell you—

No. It's been sixteen years.
I would say, *I am your witness.*

No. I have never told the whole truth.
Forgive me.

It was my first job
and I was lost in it.

SO GET OVER IT, HONEY

First bout of Shanghai flu, sweat the bed without you
First night walking west over Ellington Bridge
spy Marilyn's face in the mural over HEIDI'S LIQUOR,
yearning, so I say, *Don't kill yourself* but this is ridiculous
without you
First conversation with my mother who tells me I'm selfish
without you
First movie I see, matinee about Monk whose wife and mistress
looked after him so he could play but still he cracked, he was a
genius without you
First Dorito binge 'til my lips turn into the slugs I poured salt on
when I was a kid without you
First talk-the-talk with Dave who says you're a schmuck so I
should go get laid without you

First drive to Carolina where my cousin Mason's wife takes the
babies
and leaves the state and he crawls into detox—not easy, but simple
without you
First Christmas I wish I was Buddhist without you
First death, it was Dom, he was twenty-seven, lung cancer and that's
all I know without you
First time I tutor the kids at the shelter and say, *Tell me what you like to do*
and one says, *Go see Grandma* & the other says, *Stupid! Grandma's dead*
without you
First January thaw, I find a 1943 penny in the alley without you

First period, Oh there is a God without you

RUSSELL EDSON

Russell Edson hesitates to use the word poetry for what he writes or to even call himself a poet; instead, he thinks of his poems as fables without morals. He calls poetry a primitive pleasure enjoyed by intuitive simpletons. Many of his poems come out of his readings in science, as he tries to understand emotionally what he says his intellect can't handle. Some poets write out of personal experience, attempting to describe the world. For other poets, like Edson, the imagination and invention become the tools for naming and creating reality. Rather than depicting experience, poems for him are gestures that mimic the shape of thought. He thinks of poems as waking dreams, in that each poem is a moment of being fully conscious while tapping into the dream mind. He says his poems are about creating worlds where the dream life coincides or collides with real life, that poems create parallel realities. Compressed, almost always short, his works are exclusively in the prose poem form. He believes the shorter the work the more it can depend on symbol, metaphor, and gesture. There is an exacting precision and logic in these waking dreams. Edson says the world is a strange place, and it helps to see yourself as a secret agent. The poet is both a part of the world, engaged, but always with the meticulous focus and detachment of a spy.

ON THE EATING OF MICE

A woman was roasting a mouse for her husband's dinner; then to serve it with a blueberry in its mouth.

At table he uses a dentist's pick and a surgeon's scalpel, bending over the tiny roastling with a jeweler's loupe . . .

Twenty years of this: curried mouse; garlic and butter mouse; mouse sautéed in its own fur; Salisbury mouse; mouse-in-the-trap, baked in the very trap that killed it; mouse tartare; mouse poached in menstrual blood at the full of the moon . . .

Twenty years of this, eating their way through the mice . . . And yet, not to forget, each night one less vermin in the world . . .

COUNTING SHEEP

A scientist has a test tube full of sheep. He wonders if he should try to shrink a pasture for them.

They are like grains of rice.

He wonders if it is possible to shrink something out of existence.

He wonders if the sheep are aware of their tininess, if they have any sense of scale. Perhaps they just think the test tube is a glass barn . . .

He wonders what he should do with them; they certainly have less meat and wool than ordinary sheep. Has he reduced their commercial value?

He wonders if they could be used as a substitute for rice, a sort of woolly rice . . .

He wonders if he just shouldn't rub them into a red paste between his fingers.

He wonders if they're breeding, or if any of them have died.

He puts them under a microscope and falls asleep counting them . . .

ANTIMATTER

On the other side of a mirror there's an inverse world, where the insane go sane; where bones climb out of the earth and recede to the first slime of love.

And in the evening the sun is just rising.

Lovers cry because they are a day younger, and soon childhood robs them of their pleasure.

In such a world there is much sadness which, of course, is joy . . .

THE FALL

There was a man who found two leaves and came indoors holding them out saying to his parents that he was a tree.

To which they said then go into the yard and do not grow in the living-room as your roots may ruin the carpet.

He said I was fooling I am not a tree and he dropped his leaves.

But his parents said look it is fall.

KEVIN YOUNG

Kevin Young says writing for him is both a way of transcribing ghosts, of calling up the past, and at the same time an act of repelling those ghosts, exorcising them, or laying them to rest. Many of his poems are inspired by the paintings of Jean-Michel Basquiat, and Basquiat's themes of royalty, heroism, the street, and pop culture. He also writes many poems in the form of blues lyrics, following in the tradition of the great poet Langston Hughes. Poets are attracted to the sensibility of the blues for its humor, imagery, insinuation, and great compression—the blues can tell an epic-length story in three or four cinematic stanzas. The novelist Ralph Ellison described the blues as "an impulse to keep the painful details and episodes of a brutal experience alive in one's aching consciousness, to finger its jagged grain, and to transcend it, not by the consolation of philosophy but by squeezing from it a near-tragic, near-comic lyricism." Young describes the interior world of "Eddie Priest's Barbershop & Notary" by using external imagery from the natural world. This displacement pulls us out of everyday time into a mythic out-of-time realm. In this poem he invokes the landscape of his childhood and family.

[B L U E S]

Gimme some fruit
Gimme some fruit
Fresh salted melon
maybe some mango too

You had me eating pork ribs
You had me eatin ham
You had me so I was feedin
straight out your hand

Gimme some fruit, baby
Gimme some fru-uit
Something red
& juicy I can sink
these teeths into

You had me eatin peas Lord
You had me eatin spam
(You had me so turned round)
I never dreamt all you said
came straight out a can

Gimme some fruit
Gimme some fru-uit
Gimme something strong girl
to clear my system of you

You served me up
like chicken
You deviled me like ham
Alls the while I never knew
you had you another man

Gimme some fruit, girl
Gimme some tomato too
What else is a poor
carnivore like me
without you supposed to do

EDDIE PRIEST'S BARBERSHOP & NOTARY
Closed Mondays

is music   is men
off early from work   is waiting
for the chance at the chair
while the eagle claws holes
in your pockets   keeping
time   by the turning
of rusty fans   steel flowers with
cold breezes   is having nothing
better to do   than guess at the years
of hair   matted beneath the soiled caps
of drunks   the pain of running
a fisted comb through stubborn
knots   is the dark dirty low
down blues   the tender heads
of sons fresh from cornrows   all
wonder at losing   half their height
is a mother gathering hair   for good
luck   for a soft wig   is the round
difficulty of ears   the peach
faced boys asking Eddie
to cut in parts and arrows
wanting to have their names read

for just a few days   and among thin
jazz   is the quick brush of a done
head   the black flood around
your feet   grandfathers
stopping their games of ivory
dominoes   just before they reach the bone
yard   is winking widowers announcing
cut it clean off   I'm through courting
and hair only gets in the way   is the final
spin of the chair   a reflection of
a reflection   that sting of wintergreen
tonic   on the neck of a sleeping snow
haired man   when you realize it is
your turn   you are next

NEGATIVE

Wake to find everything black
what was white, all the vice
versa—white maids on TV, black

sitcoms that star white dwarfs
cute as pearl buttons. Black Presidents,
Black Houses. White horse

candidates. All bleach burns
clothes black. Drive roads
white as you are, white songs

on the radio stolen by black bands
like secret pancake recipes, white back-up
singers, ball-players & boxers all

white as tar. Feathers on chickens
dark as everything, boiling in the pot
that called the kettle honky. Even

whites of the eye turn dark, pupils
clear & changing as a cat's.
Is this what we've wanted

& waited for? to see snow
covering everything black
as Christmas, dark pages written

white upon? All our eclipses bright,
dark stars shooting across pale
sky, glowing like ash in fire, shower

every skin. Only money keeps
green, still grows & burns like grass
under dark daylight.

NUALA NÍ DHOMHNAILL

Praised as the most gifted Irish poet since William Butler Yeats, Nuala Ní Dhomhnaill writes in her homeland's official language, Irish. She says Irish is the language her soul speaks and allows her to access the mythic muse energy. Many of her poems come out of weaving ancient myths and folk tales with contemporary life. In this way, she creates a poetry where the magical, holy, and supernatural permeate and penetrate the profane and commonplace. For example, she has written a bardic praise poem to Prozac and another about a mermaid at the hairstylist. She says she is only interested in writing about the "biggies": birth, death, and the most important thing in between, sex. In "Nude," she humorously and lovingly overturns a long tradition of the female nude by enacting a poetic striptease on her husband. The second half of the poem echoes the language of the sensual "Song of Songs" in the Old Testament.

NUDE

The long and short
of it is I'd far rather see you nude —
your silk shirt
and natty

tie, the brolly under your oxter
in case of a rainy day,
the three-piece seersucker
suit that's so incredibly trendy,

your snazzy loafers
and, la-di-da,
a pair of gloves
made from the skin of a doe,

then, to top it all, a crombie hat
set at a rak-
ish angle — none of these add
up to more than the icing on the cake.

For, unbeknownst to the rest
of the world, behind the outward
show lies a body unsurpassed
for beauty, without so much as a wart

or blemish, but the brill-
iant slink of a wild animal, a dream-
cat, say, on the prowl,
leaving murder and mayhem

in its wake. Your broad, sinewy
shoulders and your flank
smooth as the snow
on a snow-bank.

Your back, your slender waist,
and, of course,
the root that is the very seat
of pleasure, the pleasure-source.

Your skin so dark, my beloved,
and soft
as silk with a hint of velvet
in its weft,

smelling as it does of meadowsweet
or 'watermead'
that has the power, or so it's said,
to drive men and women mad.

For that reason alone, if for no other,
when you come with me to the dance tonight
(though, as you know, I'd much prefer
to see you nude)

it would probably be best
for you to pull on your pants and vest
rather than send
half the women of Ireland totally round the bend.

TRANSLATED BY PAUL MULDOON

THE RACE

Like a mad lion, like a wild bull, like one
of the crazy pigs in the Fenian cycle
or the hero leaping upon the giant
with his fringe of swinging silk,
I drive at high speed through
the small midland towns of Ireland,
catching up with the wind ahead
while the wind behind me whirls and dies.

Like a shaft from a bow, like a shot from a gun
or a sparrow-hawk in a sparrow-throng
on a March day, I scatter the road-signs,
miles or kilometres what do I care.
Nenagh, Roscrea, Mountmellick,
I pass through them in a daze;
they are only speed limits put there
to hold me up on my way to you.

Through mountain cleft, bogland and wet pasture
I race impetuously from west to east—
a headlong flight in your direction,
a quick dash to be with you.
The road rises and falls before me,
the surface changing from grit to tar;
I forget geography, all I know
is the screech of brakes and the gleam of lights.

 Suddenly, in the mirror, I catch sight of the sun
glowing red behind me on the horizon,
a vast blazing crimson sphere like the heart
of the Great Cow of the Smith-God
when she was milked through a sieve,

the blood dripping as in a holy picture.
Thrice red, it is so fierce it pierces
my own heart, and I catch my breath in pain.

I keep glancing anxiously at the dripping sun
while trying to watch the road ahead.
So Sleeping Beauty must have glanced
at her finger after the spindle
of the spinning-wheel had pricked her,
turning it round and round as if in a trance.
When Deirdre saw the calf's blood on the snow
did it ever dawn on her what the raven was?

Oh, I know it's to you that I'm driving,
my lovely man, the friend of my heart,
and the only things between us tonight
are the road-sign and the traffic-light;
but your impatience is like a stone
dropping upon us out of the sky;
and add to that our bad humour,
gaucherie, and the weight of my terrible pride.

Another great weight is descending upon us
if things turn out as predicted, a weight
greater by far than the globe of the sun
that bled in my mirror a while back;
and thou, dark mother, cave of wonders,
since it's to you that we spin on our violent course,
is it true what they say that your kiss is sweeter
than Spanish wine, Greek honey, or the golden mead of the Norse?

TRANSLATED BY DEREK MAHON

CHARLES HARPER WEBB

Charles Harper Webb is a poet, college professor, psychotherapist, avid fly fisherman, and ex–rock and roll guitarist. His first book of poems didn't come out until he was forty. He says he learned a lot about the art of writing poetry from playing rock and roll in Seattle and Houston clubs. He learned, for example, that if you lose your audience you die, so he tries to make a poem fun and entertaining. His poems often read like compressed essays. In the poem "Tone of Voice" Webb uses the poet's tools of metaphor and simile to playfully explore the limitations—really the frustrating impossibility—a writer faces when trying to approximate on the page the whole symphony of emotion and nuance available to the human voice.

THE NEW MARRIAGE

4 / 24 / 99

It doesn't ask that either party love or honor (let alone obey),
And never mentions death; it's too depressing.

It suggests the couple likes each other well enough today,
And will tomorrow—though if not, no one's to blame.

It requests that all contracts and finances be in order.
It has written its own vows, striving for a tone of optimistic wistfulness.

It tolerates plastic cupids and wedding cake and God to please
The parents, but discourages heart-shaped soap and virgin white.

It bars from the chapel words like "obstinance," "neurosis,"
"Sulks," "downfall." At the reception, though, anything goes!

In the stories it will tell its kids, Cinderella puts on her glass slipper
And cuts an artery; Sleeping Beauty gets her kiss and a bad flu.

The ceremony celebrating it concludes with each partner mumbling,
"I guess."

TONE OF VOICE

It pinks the cheeks of speech, or flushes the forehead.
It's a spring breeze in which words play, a scorching sun
that burns them red, slate clouds that cover them in ice.
Mastering tone, the child outgrows his sticks and stones.

"Okay," he sneers, twisting the word in Mommie's eye.
Ellipses, dashes, all capitals, underlines—
these are tuna nets through which tone's minnows slide.
"I love you" may arrive spiked like a mace, or snickering.

"State your name" from lawyers' lips can mean "You lie!"
Tone leaks the truth despite our best efforts to hide.
It's verbal garlic; mistress on a husband's hands.
Consider, dear, when you ask, "Where are my French fries?"

how you may stand in a silk teddy holding grapes,
a suit of mail holding a lance, a hangman's hood holding
a rope. As useless to protest, "I didn't mean that,"
as to tell a corpse, "Stand up. You misinterpreted my car."

BUYER'S REMORSE

I'd hate to take a job teaching, then spend
my life trying to get out of it.
                                    —Mary Oliver

No sooner do the ruck of us declare
"I do," than we don't anymore. Go out
for football, and we who never dared
to stand up on a pair of ice skates, pout
that we can't play pro hockey too. The ink's
still wet on our tickets to France, and we
wish we'd picked Japan or, come to think
of it, Kauai, New Zealand, or Tahiti.
Open any one door and we're deafened
by the roar—loud as the sea swallowing Atlantis—
as other doors slam shut, and their wind
knocks us down. The serpent didn't hiss
    to Adam and Eve, "Hide your nakedness!"
    He wore his best suit, and whispered, "Look at this."

DENISE DUHAMEL

While Denise Duhamel lived in New York City in the 80s she was robbed three times. To fight the despair and panic, she custom ordered a neon sign that spelled out the word "poet" in hot pink cursive and hung it from her bedroom window, where it flashed all night. It was during this time that the most popular doll of the twentieth century, Barbie, drove her Cadillac right up Avenue D and into Duhamel's imagination. Buddhist Barbie, Twelve Step Barbie, Hippie Barbie: Duhamel takes the icons of contemporary life out of their fairy-tale facades and into the world of real women and men. Having spent several years writing for stand-up comedians, she brings elements of comedy to her poems, revealing hard truths about our culture with great humor and bite.

HIPPIE BARBIE

Barbie couldn't grasp the concept
of free love. After all, she was born
into the world of capitalism
where nothing is free. And all she had
to choose from was a blond or dark-haired Ken
who looked exactly like Midge's boyfriend Alan.
Ken wouldn't even get bell-bottoms
or his first psychedelic pantsuit
until it was way too late, sometime in the mid-seventies.
And then, whenever Barbie tried to kiss him
his peel-off lamb-chop sideburns loosened
and stuck to her cheeks. There were no black male dolls yet
so she guessed a mixed-race love-child
was out of the question. Barbie walked her poodle
past the groovy chicks who showed their bellybuttons
and demonstrated against the war. She couldn't
make a peace sign with her stuck-together fingers.
She felt a little like Sandra Dee at a Janis Joplin concert.

BARBIE JOINS A TWELVE STEP PROGRAM

Barbie is *bottoming out,*
she's sitting on the *pity pot.* She hasn't the know-how to express
any of her emotions. Before she even gets
to her first meeting, she takes the first step, admits
her life *has become unmanageable.*
She's been kidnapped by boys
and tortured with pins. She's been left
for months at a time between scratchy couch cushions
with cracker crumbs, pens, and loose change.

She can't help herself from being a fashion doll.
She is the ultimate victim.

She humbly sits on a folding chair
in a damp church basement. The cigarette smoke
clouds the faces around her, the smell of bad coffee
permeates the air. The group booms the serenity prayer:
God, grant me serenity to accept the things I cannot change,
courage to change the things I can, and wisdom
to know the difference. Poor Barbie is lost
in a philosophical quandary. Her God must be Mattel.
How can she *turn her life and will over* to a toy company?
Must she accept her primary form of locomotion
being the fists of young careless humans?

And what can she change? The only reason Barbie
is at the meeting at all is because she wound up in the tote bag
of a busy mother. She toppled out when the woman,
putting on lipstick at the bathroom mirror, spilled the contents
of her bag onto the floor. The mother didn't see Barbie skid under
           a stall door
where a confused drunk, at the meeting for warmth,
was peeing. *Never thought Barbie had problems,*
she said, picking up the doll. She thought it would be funny
to prop Barbie in the last row. No one else noticed the doll
as she fidgeted in her seat. The hungry drunk
went on to spoon a cupful of sugar into her coffee.

Barbie sat through the meeting, wondering:
What is wisdom? What is letting go?
She wished she could clap like the others
when there was a good story about recovery. She accepted
she couldn't, hoping that if she stopped struggling,
her higher power, Mattel, would finally let her move.

Miracles don't happen overnight, said a speaker.
Take the action and leave the rest to God, said another.
Barbie's prayer that she would be at the next meeting was answered.
A member of the clean-up committee squished her between the seat
and back of the folding chair and stacked her, with the others, against
        the wall.

BUDDHIST BARBIE
   —for Nick

In the 5th century B.C.
an Indian philosopher Gautama
teaches "All is emptiness"
and "There is no self."
In the 20th century A.D.
Barbie agrees, but wonders how a man
with such a belly could pose,
smiling, and without a shirt.

YUSEF KOMUNYAKAA

Yusef Komunyakaa says that as a child he spent hours in a tiny library in Bogalusa, Louisiana, reading Yeats and Harlem Renaissance poets, but he said his greatest lessons in poetry came from his father who was a carpenter with little education. He says his father taught him how the unfinished can be shaped and transformed through precision and the rhythms of hard work—that what is original, rare, and beautiful is to be found in the details. Taking his father's lessons to heart, Komunyakaa shapes, polishes, and hones difficult memories and emotions so that his poems become "made things." His poems bear severe witness to having grown up in the South and served in the Vietnam War. Many of his poems are happy-sad songs. Read "Venus's-flytraps" out loud twice: in one reading it can be very funny, in another it is sad and heartbreaking. He says that poetry is an act of nonmathematical creation driven by passion, only adhering to the metrics of the heart.

ANODYNE

I love how it swells
into a temple where it is
held prisoner, where the god
of blame resides. I love
slopes & peaks, the secret
paths that make me selfish.
I love my crooked feet
shaped by vanity & work
shoes made to outlast
belief. The hardness
coupling milk it can't
fashion. I love the lips,
salt & honeycomb on the tongue.
The hair holding off rain
& snow. The white moons
on my fingernails. I love
how everything begs
blood into song & prayer
inside an egg. A ghost
hums through my bones
like Pan's midnight flute
shaping internal laws
beside a troubled river.
I love this body
made to weather the storm
in the brain, raised
out of the deep smell
of fish & water hyacinth,
out of rapture & the first
regret. I love my big hands.
I love it clear down to the soft
quick motor of each breath,

the liver's ten kinds of desire
& the kidney's lust for sugar.
This skin, this sac of dung
& joy, this spleen floating
like a compass needle inside
nighttime, always divining
West Africa's dusty horizon.
I love the birthmark
posed like a fighting cock
on my right shoulder blade.
I love this body, this
solo & ragtime jubilee
behind the left nipple,
because I know I was born
to wear out at least
one hundred angels.

THE DECK

I have almost nailed my left thumb to the 2 x 4 brace that holds the deck together. This Saturday morning in June, I have sawed 2 x 6s, T-squared and levelled everything with three bubbles sealed in green glass, and now the sweat on my tongue tastes like what I am. I know I'm alone, using leverage to swing the long boards into place, but at times it seems as if there are two of us working side by side like old lovers guessing each other's moves.

This hammer is the only thing I own of yours, and it makes me feel I have carpentered for years. Even the crooked nails are going in straight. The handsaw glides through grease. The toenailed stubs hold. The deck has risen up around me, and now it's strong enough to support my weight, to not sway with this old, silly, wrong-footed dance I'm about to throw my whole body into.

Plumbed from sky to ground, this morning's work can take nearly anything! With so much uproar and punishment, footwork and euphoria, I'm almost happy this Saturday.

I walk back inside and here you are. Plain and simple as the sunlight on the tools outside. Daddy, if you'd come back a week ago, or day before yesterday, I would have been ready to sit down and have a long talk with you. There were things I wanted to say. So many questions I wanted to ask, but now they've been answered with as much salt and truth as we can expect from the living.

VENUS'S-FLYTRAPS

I am five,
    Wading out into deep
        Sunny grass,
Unmindful of snakes
    & yellowjackets, out
        To the yellow flowers
Quivering in sluggish heat.
    Don't mess with me
        'Cause I have my Lone Ranger
Six-shooter. I can hurt
    You with questions
        Like silver bullets.
The tall flowers in my dreams are
    Big as the First State Bank,
        & they eat all the people

Except the ones I love.
   They have women's names,
      With mouths like where
Babies come from. I am five.
   I'll dance for you
      If you close your eyes. No
Peeping through your fingers.
   I don't supposed to be
      This close to the tracks.
One afternoon I saw
   What a train did to a cow.
      Sometimes I stand so close
I can see the eyes
   Of men hiding in boxcars.
      Sometimes they wave
& holler for me to get back. I laugh
   When trains make the dogs
      Howl. Their ears hurt.
I also know bees
   Can't live without flowers.
      I wonder why Daddy
Calls Mama honey.
   All the bees in the world
      Live in little white houses
Except the ones in these flowers.
   All sticky & sweet inside.
      I wonder what death tastes like.
Sometimes I toss the butterflies
   Back into the air.
      I wish I knew why
The music in my head
   Makes me scared.
      But I know things

I don't supposed to know.
  I could start walking
    & never stop.
These yellow flowers
  Go on forever.
    Almost to Detroit.
Almost to the sea.
  My mama says I'm a mistake.
    That I made her a bad girl.
My playhouse is underneath
  Our house, & I hear people
    Telling each other secrets.

HAL SIROWITZ

Famous for his "Mother said" poems, Hal Sirowitz, a special educa-
tion teacher in Queens, can be heard reading his poems on the
lower east side of Manhattan or in the cosmetics department of
Neiman Marcus on Mother's Day. I like to think of him as the
Kafka of Flushing, Queens. Sirowitz composes macabre miniatures
on family values. With a comic's dead-on, deadpan delivery he spins
out heartbreaking and hilarious poems that are wise and devastating
at the same time.

TWO VISITS IN ONE DAY

We're going to the cemetery to visit
some dead relatives, Mother said, & on the way
back we'll stop over at your aunt's house.
It's good practice to mix the living
with the dead. Otherwise, we'd end up
either being bored at the cemetery, or if
we stayed too long at her house, we'd wish
that she was dead. This way by doing
two things in one day we can do something fun
the next weekend, like go to the beach.
If your aunt keeps talking too much, like she
usually does, we'll tell her that we just got
back from the cemetery, & that should shut her up.
She never goes there, & it shows, because
the more you visit the dead the less you have to say.

HORNS ON YOUR HEAD

The further you venture from the house,
Mother said, the less people you'll know.
Everyone on this block has either heard
of you or has seen you at one time. But
on the next block maybe only one person
will recognize you. Then there are hundreds
of blocks where no one knows you exist.
And it goes on that way until you get
to Nebraska, where it gets even worse.
There, the people never met a Jew before.
They think you have horns, & will want

to look for them. That's why you should never move
too far away from me. You don't want
strangers to always be touching your head.

CRUMBS

Don't eat any food in your room,
Mother said. You'll get more bugs.
They depend on people like you.
Otherwise, they would starve.
But who do you want to make happy,
your mother or a bunch of ants?
What have they done for you?
Nothing. They have no feelings.
They'll eat your candy. Yet
you treat them better than you treat me.
You keep feeding them.
But you never offer me anything.

WORD POWER

I could have tried to have another son,
Mother said, but then I'd have to divide
my love in two, so I sacrificed,
& just had you. But sometimes I think
you could have used the competition
that a baby brother would have brought.
All the relatives would put him in their arms,
& hold him high over their heads. And that just might
stir you to action. Because right now

you're even too lazy to look up a word
in the dictionary, & your vocabulary is limited.
And one day your wife is going to ask you
if you really love her. And you should
tell her yes, & that you also idolize her.
But since you don't know what that word means,
you won't be able to use it. And even if
she buys you *Webster's Unabridged Dictionary*
for a birthday present, you still might not get the hint.

LUCIA PERILLO

Lucia Perillo came to the writing of poetry after years of working as a park ranger and biological researcher. She took her first writing class at night school with Robert Hass while working as a naturalist at the San Francisco Wildlife Reserve. While many of her poems explore her love of the natural world and her battle with multiple sclerosis, her main interest, she says, is exploring the places where culture, history, and memory intersect.

COMPULSORY TRAVEL

Not yet did we have personalities to interfere
with what we were: two sisters, two brothers.
Maybe our parents really were people who walked in the world,
were mean or kind, but you'd have to prove it to us.
They were the keepers of money, the signers of report cards,
the drivers of cars. We had a station wagon.
Back home we even had a dog, who was fed
by a neighbor kid while we toured the Jersey shore.
We waded in the motel pool and clung
to the edge of the deep end, because we couldn't swim.
Maybe that's why we never went in the ocean, despite
hours of driving. We could've just gone down the block!
Yet each year we made a ritual of this week
spent yelling and cursing and swatting each other,
with none of the analyses we now employ, the past
used as ammunition, the glosses from our latest therapist.
Back then a sock in the jaw could set anyone straight.

On Sunday afternoon, the homeward traffic would grind still
where the turnpike bottlenecked. My father
would slam his forehead against the steering wheel,
start changing lanes and leaning on the horn.
Without breeze through the window, the car would hold
our body heat like an iron skillet, skin peeling
from our burned shoulders as we hurled pretzels
and gave the finger to kids stopped in cars beside us.
My mother wouldn't mention the turn we'd missed
a few miles back; instead she'd fold the map
and jam it resolutely in the glove box while we crept on.
Perhaps this was our finest hour, as the people
we were becoming took shape and began to emerge:
the honkers of horns and the givers of fingers.

After the sun turned red and disappeared, we rolled
through darkness, wondering if the world knew all its names:
Wickatunk, Colts Neck, Zarephath, Spotswood—in every town
there were houses, in every house a light.

LOST INNOCENCE OF THE POTATO GIVERS

They're just a passing phase. All are symptoms
of our times and the confusion around us.
   —Reverend Billy Graham on The Beatles

At first we culled our winnings from the offering
     of fists—
one potato, two potato—until we realized that such
     random calibration
was no real test of love. So we cultivated pain:
     hunkering on the macadam
sun-baked for hours in the schoolyard, our panties
     bunched beneath our skirts.
The girl who could sit there longest would gain title
     to the most handsome Beatle, Paul.
John George Ringo—the rest were divvied according to
     whose buttocks were most scarlet.
And when our fourth-grade teacher asked why we wore such
     tortured looks through long division,
we shrugged, scritching our pencils over fleshy shapes
     of hearts and flowers.

Ed Sullivan started it, his chiseled and skeletal stub
     of a head, his big shoe
stomping our loyalties to the man-boys, Dion
     and Presley.

Even priggish neighbor Emily said I had to kneel before
　　　the TV as though praying.
Then the pixels assembled the audience's exploding
　　　like a carcass when it's knifed,
and I copied the pose assumed on-screen: hands pressed
　　　against sides of my skull
like the bald dwarf who stands goggle-eyed on a jetty
　　　in Munch's painting, and screams.
My mother rushed to the basement, a dishrag dripping
　　　from her soaped hand.
What's wrong? she yelled. *Are you hurt? What in godsname*
　　　is all this screaming?

February 1964: Johnson's choppers were whopping up the sky
　　　over the Gulf of Tonkin.
Despite the tacit code of silence about the war, somehow
　　　they must have known:
on television, girls were brawling drunkenly and raking
　　　fingernails across their cheeks,
ripping their own hair in vicious chunks, as though beauty
　　　were suddenly indulgent or profane.
That night in Saigon's Capital Kinh-Do Theatre, three GIs
　　　got blown up during a strip show.
But of course I didn't know that. I couldn't have even
　　　found Saigon on a map.
Girls were going limp in the arms of riot-geared policemen,
　　　who carried them off like the dead,
and my mother was stunned when she saw I'd torn my shirt
　　　over my not-yet-breasts.

After that, I kept everything a secret, the self-inflicted
　　　burns and scars and nicks.
I was doing it for love love love: the stones in my shoes,
　　　the burrs in my shirt,

the mother-of-pearl penknife I used for cutting grooves
    in my thumb or palm
whenever I needed to swear some blood pact with another
    disenthralled potato giver.
We spent recess practicing how to stick our tongues
    in Paul's imaginary mouth,
letting everything drain out until we were limp, nothing,
    sucked right into the earth.
Then we would mash our bodies against the schoolyard's wide
    and gray-barked beech,
which was cruel and strong and unrelenting, smooth and cold,
    the way we hoped our husbands would be.

AMY GERSTLER

In a tell-all "talk show" culture that commodifies intimacy and the spiritual, poets must constantly discover alternative strategies to undermine and subvert the mass production of the self. One strategy Amy Gerstler uses is fashioning what she calls "Fake Autobiographies," showing how a self-portrait can be revealed as much through imagination and invention as through direct confession. In her poetry we often find an anti-aesthetic at work, where meaning and beauty can be found in the odds and ends, the detritus, and the discarded. She describes her muse this way: "His filament-thin smile / is the type often seen / on the lips of an infant / with a full bladder, or gas. / Or, his smirk can resemble / the jerky, erratic line / of an electrocardiogram, / sketched in between / the nose and chin / of a young mother." Gerstler's postmodern prayer "Modern Madonnas" is a haunting litany of contemporary suffering.

MODERN MADONNAS

Our lady of immunology.
Madonna of feline leukemia.
Our lady of unpaid anesthesiologist bills.
Virgin of earthquakes on the fortieth floor.
Our lady of diabetic blindness.
Madonna of drudgery.
Our lady of deadpan.
Our lady of drive-by shootings.
Madonna of laboratory animals.
Virgin of the safety deposit box.
Our lady of the sales pitch.
Heavy-lidded Madonna of thorazine.
Virgin of planetary tensions.
Personal virgin of stainless steel.
Madonna of the iron lung.
Madonna of the stock market.
Our lady of the statewide blackout.
Madonna of radiation sickness.
Madonna of carbon monoxide.
Our lady of genetic mutation.
Virgin of ether.
Madonna of nitroglycerin.
Virgin of medical ethics.
Our lady of instant cremation.
Our lady of concentration camps.
Madonna of poisoned aspirin.
Our lady of the sniper at the elementary school.
Virgin of the dwindling emergency rooms.
Madonna of the negative horizon.
Madonna of technology.
Madonna of the mass media.
Our lady's machine museum.

Virgin of the revelation of identity.
Madonna of the double-blind study.
Our lady of AZT.
Our lady of psychoanalysis.
Virgin of computer-engineered tax evasion.
Madonna of the synchronized sound track.
Madonna of autonomy.
Our lady of Dianetics.
Our lady of the stalled escalator.
Virgin of food irradiation.
Virgin of chemically induced birth defects.
Madonna of the wildcat strike.
Our lady of cigarette advertising.
Our lady of twilight sleep.
Madonna of suits "made by some poor slob in Hong Kong."
Virgin of the extra "Y" chromosome.
Madonna of fossil fuels.
Madonna of gridlock.
Virgin of the complete blood transfusion.
Virgin of sudden infant death syndrome.
Our lady of organ transplants.
Our lady of the power lunch.
Madonna of after-hours clubs.
Virgin of the oil glut.
Our lady of talk radio.
Madonna of the Gallup Poll.
Madonna of Muzak and call-waiting.
Our lady of sexual harassment.
Madonna of the glib interviewer.
Our lady of the temporal lobe.
Madonna of the caste system.
Our lady of unpaid sick leave.
Madonna of infinite echolalia.

HER ACCOUNT OF HERSELF

Born at the onset
of this tranquilizer age,
I spent decades awakening,
wandering this nation's
dazzling displays
of petticoats and neckties.
I grew into a needle-nosed
scribbler, a tight-lipped
wallflower seated between
lively philistines at banquets
and sacrifices. Such am I:
a barren head-hanger,
a secret rabbit breeder,
addicted to bonbons
and collecting botanically
accurate hand-tinted
etchings of flowering cacti
since time out of mind.
I kept my legs crossed
just as instructed,
for a hideously long time.
I still have trouble telling
the difference between
progress and pathology,
hate getting my face wet,
will not eat banana squash,
learned to ride a bike
at twenty, experience
difficulty warming up.
Were there a museum of me,
it might contain my fur muff,
my pup's first leather collar,

necklaces I made as a child
by stringing watermelon seeds,
my hearing aid, five mother-
of-pearl buttons from my unhappy
grandmother's blouse
(she never wanted to marry,
but got pregnant, and that
was that), a lopped-off ponytail,
a red eucalyptus leaf
that stuck to the windshield
of one I unsuccessfully loved,
my pocket watch, and the tub of
sweet grease I use
to groom my terrible hair.
I've often sought asylum,
remained unseduced by food,
planted a kiss on the wall
by the landing where the turn
in the stairs is called
the "coffin corner."
I'm nothing if not
cheerfully morbid, or so
my friends claim.
Call upon me if you need
contact with that breezy,
self-conscious type of turmoil
that chases its tail all day,
forming little whirlwinds.

MY MUSE

His filament-thin smile
is the type often seen
on the lips of an infant
with a full bladder, or gas.
Or, his smirk can resemble
the jerky, erratic line
of an electrocardiogram,
sketched in between
the nose and chin
of a young mother
who's just learned
she's got heart
trouble. This muse
never received proper
dental care when young.
Consequently, some of his
teeth have "jumped ship" —
his quaint phrase.
Unforgiving as blisters,
he's as wretched
as the skinny magician's
assistant he invented
to weigh on my mind.
She lies quietly
in her false coffin,
only her head and feet
visible. She tries
to relax while her tuxedoed
boss, a sweaty, uncertain
man who doesn't know chalk
from cheese, proceeds
to saw her in half.

MAURA STANTON

Maura Stanton grew up in the 50s on the edge of Peoria, a place advertised as the most modern community in central Illinois, and which consisted of tract after tract of identical bungalows—a world she describes as beige on beige. In this world, and later in Minnesota where her family moved, she said she really had to develop her imagination and dream of a multi-hued, vibrant life of world travel while working part-time and going to college. While in college she took a poetry writing class that changed her life. She wrote 125 poems that quarter, trying not to wake her two-year-old sister with whom she shared a room. In "Childhood" she starts out by describing a game she used to play as a child, where she would lie on the floor and look up and imagine that she was walking on the ceiling. In the second half of the poem, Stanton turns that game into a metaphor about the way we as adults can completely lose our ability to see from other perspectives in a childlike, imaginative way.

GIFTS

Lilac, lavender, lily of the valley—
I lift the soap up to my face.
I'm Christmas shopping for my aunt,
who's forced to discontinue chemo,
hardly able to keep food down.
I used to send her panettone,
boxes of glazed apricots,
or lavish travel books on Ireland—
things I thought a nun would like
to unwrap after Midnight mass.
But the many worldly objects
I've fingered in a dozen shops—
hand blown glass, engagement books,
tote bags stenciled with sleeping cats—
seemed so wrong I stepped into
this fragrance store for inspiration.
And yet a wave of guilt chokes me
as I give my credit card to a clerk
for this little stack of boxes,
wildflowers sealed in glycerin,
hand-milled distilled carnations,
lanolin ovals of English violet.
Is this to be my final gift?
The clerk hands the card back.
My thumb runs over the numbers
embossed on the slick front,
and with a tingle I remember
stroking my aunt's holy cards
enclosed with childhood birthday presents,
pictures of Mary dressed in blue
bending over the swaddled child,
or martyrs smiling serenely

from the rack, their legs broken.
My favorite scene was Jesus
surprising his mother in the Temple,
his expression rapt and tender
as he taught the amazed elders.
I'd stroke the textured halos
around the sacred heads, as if
sanctity might rub off on me
absorbed through my human skin.
Now it's only money's ghost
I touch, slipping my card
back with others into my wallet,
before I grab the paper bag
off the glass counter, hoping
in spite of my devouring gloom
that my aunt's face is shining
like the saints, that this soap
smells to her of heavenly gardens.

for Sr. Coletta M. Stanton, BVM
1922–1994

CHILDHOOD

I used to lie on my back, imagining
A reverse house on the ceiling of my house
Where I could walk around in empty rooms
All by myself. There was no furniture
Up there, only a glass globe in the floor,
And knee-high barriers at every door.
The low silled windows opened on blue air.
Nothing hung in the closet; even the kitchen

Seemed immaculate, a place for thought.
I liked to walk across the swirling plaster
Into the parts of the house I couldn't see.
The hum from the other house, now my ceiling,
Reached me only faintly. I'd look up
To find my brothers watching old cartoons,
Or my mother vacuuming the ugly carpet.
I'd stare amazed at unmade beds, the clutter,
Shoes, half-dressed dolls, the telephone,
Then return dizzily to my perfect floorplan
Where I never spoke or listened to anyone.

I must have turned down the wrong hall,
Or opened a door that locked shut behind me,
For I live on the ceiling now, not the floor.
This is my house, room after empty room.
How do I ever get back to the real house
Where my sisters spill milk, my father calls,
And I am at the table, eating cereal?
I fill my white rooms with furniture,
Hang curtains over the piercing blue outside.
I lie on my back. I strive to look down.
This ceiling is higher than it used to be,
The floor so far away I can't determine
Which room I'm in, which year, which life.

MAPLE TREE

One day an old man turned his yellow eye
Upon our maple tree, & climbed & climbed
Until his grey coat shook like a squirrel's tail
Above the black hats of the fire brigade
& dancing children, shouting, Fly! Oh, fly!
Wedged in a high crook, his heart bloomed
For the last time; smothered in army blankets
Hand to hand they passed him down the ladder.
Now I remember how his waiting family
Turned, ashamed, to the ambulance,
While neighbors kicked the tree, then, looking up,
Traced their whorled thumbs along the living bark
As if the trunk were braille, & some clear thing
I couldn't understand was growing there.

MARILYN CHIN

Marilyn Chin calls herself a comparatist; she sees her poems as hybrids of the past and present as she weaves in diverse traditions and voices—from Shakespeare, to rap, to ancient Chinese poetic forms. She says her poems are places to heal the bloody past. In an America that is not monolithic and monolingual, an America of many songs and many tribes, Chin, born in Hong Kong and raised in Portland, believes the role of the poet is to be the conduit of many voices—the singer of many songs. As comfortable with a scratch track as a haiku, she writes poems that read like multilayered, multitongued chromatics that get to the heart of assimilation, exile, and identity. Chin says "Song of the Sad Guitar" is her attempt at a haibun, a Japanese essay poem form that she punctuates with fits of verse. She remakes a character from the Tang Dynasty into a contemporary hippie California muse. "Rhapsody in Plain Yellow" mimics the ancient Fu form, characterized by long exposition, incantation, and wild, ornate associative imagery, often performed by a shaman. In "The Floral Apron" she takes an everyday domestic garment and turns it into a priestly, sacred robe, in the same way that poetry makes us see the common and ordinary in new, extraordinary ways.

THE FLORAL APRON

The woman wore a floral apron around her neck,
that woman from my mother's village
with a sharp cleaver in her hand.
She said, "What shall we cook tonight?
Perhaps these six tiny squid
lined up so perfectly on the block?"

She wiped her hand on the apron,
pierced the blade into the first.
There was no resistance,
no blood, only cartilage
soft as a child's nose. A last
iota of ink made us wince.

Suddenly, the aroma of ginger and scallion fogged our senses,
and we absolved her for that moment's barbarism.
Then, she, an elder of the tribe,
without formal headdress, without elegance,
deigned to teach the younger
about the Asian plight.

And although we have traveled far
we would never forget that primal lesson
—on patience, courage, forbearance,
on how to love squid despite squid,
how to honor the village, the tribe,
that floral apron.

SONG OF THE SAD GUITAR

In the bitter year of 1988 I was banished to San Diego, California, to become a wife there. It was summer. I was buying groceries under the Yin and Yang sign of Safeway. In the parking lot, the puppies were howling to a familiar tune on a guitar plucked with the zest and angst of the sixties. I asked the player her name.

She answered:
   "Stone Orchid, but if you call me that, I'll kill you."
I said:
   "Yes, perhaps stone is too harsh for one with a voice so pure."
She said:
   "It's the 'orchid' I detest; it's prissy, cliché and forever pink."

From my shopping bag I handed her a Tsing Tao and urged her to play on.

She sang about hitchhiking around the country, moons and lakes, homeward-honking geese, scholars who failed the examination. Men leaving for war; women climbing the watchtower. There were courts, more courts and inner-most courts, and scions who pillaged the country.

Suddenly, I began to feel deeply about my own banishment. The singer I could have been, what the world looked like in spring, that Motown collection I lost. I urged her to play on:

Trickle, Trickle, the falling rain.
Ming, ming, a deer lost in the forest.
Surru, surru, a secret conversation.
Hung, hung, a dog in the yard.

Then, she changed her mood, to a slower lament, trilled a song macabre, about death, about a guitar case that opened like a coffin. Each string vibrant, each note a thought. Tell me, Orchid, where are we going? "The book of changes does not signify change. The laws are immutable. Our fates are sealed." Said Orchid—the song is a dirge and an awakening.

Two years after our meeting, I became deranged. I couldn't cook, couldn't clean. My house turned into a pigsty. My children became delinquents. My husband began a long lusty affair with another woman. The house burned during a feverish *Santa Ana* as I sat in a pink cranny above the garage singing, "At twenty, I marry you. At thirty, I begin hating everything that you do."

One day while I was driving down Mulberry Lane, a voice came over the radio. It was Stone Orchid. She said, "This is a song for an old friend of mine. Her name is Mei Ling. She's a warm and sensitive housewife now living in Hell's Creek, California. I've dedicated this special song for her, 'The Song of the Sad Guitar.'"

I am now beginning to understand the song within the song, the weeping within the willow. And you, out there, walking, talking, seemingly alive—may truly be dead and waiting to be summoned by the sound of the sad guitar.

for Maxine Hong Kingston

RHAPSODY IN PLAIN YELLOW

For my love, Charles (1938–2000)

Say: 言

I love you, I love you, I love you, no matter
    your race, your sex, your color. Say:
the world is round and the arctic is cold.
    Say: I shall kiss the rondure of your soul's
living marl. Say: he is beautiful,
    serenely beautiful, yet, only ephemerally so.
Say: Her Majesty combs her long black hair for hours.
    Say: O rainbows, in his eyes, rainbows.
Say: O frills and fronds, I know you
    Mr. Snail Consciousness,
O foot plodding the underside of leaves.
    Say: I am nothing without you, nothing,
Ms. Lookeast, Ms. Lookeast,
    without you, I am utterly empty.
Say: the small throat of sorrow.
    Say: China and France, China and France.
Say: Beauty and loss, the dross of centuries.
    Say: Nothing in their feudal antechamber
shall relinquish us of our beauty—
    Say: Mimosa—this is not a marriage song (epithalamion).
Say: when I was a young girl in Hong Kong
    a prince came on a horse, I believe it was piebald.
O dead prince   dead dead prince   who paid for my ardor.
    Say: O foot   O ague   O warbling oratorio . . .
Say: Darling, use "love" only as a transitive verb
    for the first forty years of your life.
Say: I have felt this before, it's soft, human.
    Say: my love is a fragile concertina.

Say: you always love them in the beginning,
　then, you take them to slaughter.
O her coarse whispers　O her soft bangs.
　By their withers, they are emblazoned doppelgangers.
Say: beauty and terror, beauty and terror.
　Say: the house is filled with perfume,
dancing sonatinas and pungent flowers.
　Say: houses filled with combs　combs　combs
and the mistress' wan ankles.
　Say: embrace the An Lu Shan ascendancy
and the fantastical diaspora of tears.
　Say: down blue margins
my inky love runs. Tearfully,
　tearfully, the pearl concubine runs.
There is a tear in his left eye—sadness or debris?
　Say: reverence to her, reverence to her.
Say: I am a very small boy, a very small boy,
　I am a teeny weeny little boy
who yearns to be punished.
　Say, I can't live without you
Head Mistress, Head Mistress,
　I am a little lamb, a consenting little lamb,
I am a sheep without his fold.
　Say: God does not exist and hell is other people—
and Mabel, can't we get out of this hotel?
　Say: Gregor Samsa—someone in Tuscaloosa
thinks you're *magnifico*, she will kiss
　your battered cheek, embrace your broken skull.
Is the apple half eaten or half whole?
　Suddenly, he moves within me, how do I know
that he is not death, in death there is

　certain // caesura.

Say: there is poetry in his body, poetry
   in his body, yes, say:
this dead love, this dead love,
   this dead, dead love, this lovely death,
this white percale, white of hell, of heavenly shale.
   Centerfolia . . . say: kiss her sweet lips.
Say: what rhymes with "flower":
   "bower," "shower," "power"?
I am that yellow girl, that famished yellow girl
   from the first world.
Say: I don't give a shit about nothing
   'xcept my cat, your cock and poetry.
Say: a refuge between sleeping and dying.
   Say: to Maui   to Maui   to Maui
creeps in his petty pompadour.
   Day to day, her milk of human kindness
ran dry; I shall die of   jejune jejune   *la lune la lune.*
   Say: a beleaguered soldier, a fine arse had he.
Say: I have seen the small men of my generation
   rabid, discrete, hysterical, lilliput, naked.
Say: Friday is okay; we'll have fish.
   Say: Friday is not okay; he shall die
of the measles near the bay.
   Say: Friday, just another savage
day until Saturday, the true Sabbath, when they shall
   finally stay.   Say:
                 Sojourner
                      Truth.
Say: I am dismayed by your cloying promiscuousness
   and fawning attitude.
Say: *amaduofu, amaduofu.*
   Say: he put cumin and tarragon in his stew.
Say: he's the last wave of French Algerian Jews.
   He's a cousin of Helene Cixous, twice removed.

Say: he recites the lost autobiography of Camus.
    Say: I am a professor from the University of Stupidity,
I cashed my welfare check and felt good.
    I saw your mama crossing the bridge of magpies
up on the faded hillock with the Lame Ox—
    Your father was conspicuously absent.
Admit that you loved your mother,
    that you killed your father to marry your mother.
Suddenly, my terrible childhood made sense.
    Say: beauty and truth, beauty and truth,
all ye need to know on earth all ye need to know.
    Say: I was boogying down, boogying down
Victoria Peak Way and a slip-of-a-boy climbed off his ox;
    he importuned me for a kiss, a tiny one
on his cankered lip.
    Say: O celebrator   O celebrant
of a blessed life, say:
    false   fleeting   hopes
Say: despair, despair, despair.
    Say: Chinawoman, I am a contradiction in terms:
I embody frugality and ecstasy.
    Friday Wong died on a Tuesday,
O how he loved his lambs.
    He was lost in their sheepfold.
Say: another mai tai before your death.
    Another measure   another murmur   before your last breath.
Another boyfriend, Italianesque.
    Say: Save. Exit.
Say: I am the sentence which shall at last elude her.
    Oh, the hell of heaven's girth, a low mound from here . . .
Say:
    Oh, a mother's vision of the emerald hills draws down her brows.
Say: A brush of jade, a jasper plow furrow.
    Say: ####oooooxxxxx!!!!

Contemplate   thangs   cerebral   spiritual   open   stuff   reality
    by definition   lack   any   spatial   extension
we occupy   no space   and   are   not   measurable
    we do not move   undulate   are not in   perpetual motion
where   for example   is thinking   in the head?   in my vulva?

    whereas   in my female lack of penis?   Physical
thangs   spatial extensions   mathematically   measurable
    preternaturally   possible   lack bestial   vegetable   consciousness
lack   happiness   lackluster   lack   *chutzpah*   lack   love

Say: A scentless camellia bush bloodied the afternoon.
    Fuck this line, can you really believe this?
When did I become the master of suburban bliss?
    With whose tongue were we born?
The language of the masters is the language of the aggressors.
    We've studied their cadence carefully—
enrolled in a class to *improve our accent.*
    Meanwhile, they hover over, waiting for us to stumble . . .
to drop an article, mispronounce an R.
    Say: softly, softly, the silent gunboats glide.
O onerous sibilants, O onomatopoetic glibness.
    Say:
How could we write poetry in a time like this?
    A discipline that makes much ado about so little?
Willfully laconic, deceptively disguised as a love poem.

Say:
your engorging dict-
atorial flesh
grazed mine.

Would you have loved me more if I were black?
　　Would I have loved you more if you were white?
And you, relentless Sinophile,
　　holding my long hair, my frayed dreams.

My turn to objectify you.
　　I, the lunatic, the lover, the poet,
the face of an orphan static with flies,
　　the scourge of the old world,
which reminds us—it ain't all randy dandy
　　in the new kingdom.

Say   rebuke   descry

Hills and canyons, robbed by sun, leave us nothing.

PHILIP BOOTH

Philip Booth lives in the same house that his family has shared for five generations in the tiny seaside village of Castine, Maine. In one poem he claims, "I'm puritan to the bone, down / to the marrow and then some: / if I'm sorry I worry, if I can't worry I count." A student of Robert Frost, he says that poetry teaches us to survive, both spiritually and sometimes literally. Booth says that a nun told him she was once swept away by strong Atlantic currents beyond the sight of the lifeguards, and as she was trying to keep her composure, instead of a prayer, she recited the words of Booth's poem "First Lesson" over and over to herself. Poets often give advice, and there is an explicit instruction in this poem—we all know it is dangerous to fight the currents in the ocean—but it is a metaphorical instruction as well. He believes that every poem, every work of art, every thing that is well-made, well-said, generously given, adds to our chances of survival by making the world and our lives more habitable.

HOPE

Old spirit, in and beyond me,
keep and extend me. Amid strangers,
friends, great trees and big seas breaking,
let love move me. Let me hear the whole music,
see clear, reach deep. Open me to find due words,
that I may shape them to ploughshares of my own making.
After such luck, however late, give me to give to
the oldest dance. . . . Then to good sleep,
and—if it happens—glad waking.

FIRST LESSON

Lie back, daughter, let your head
be tipped back in the cup of my hand.
Gently, and I will hold you. Spread
your arms wide, lie out on the stream
and look high at the gulls. A dead-
man's-float is face down. You will dive
and swim soon enough where this tidewater
ebbs to the sea. Daughter, believe
me, when you tire on the long thrash
to your island, lie up, and survive.
As you float now, where I held you
and let go, remember when fear
cramps your heart what I told you:
lie gently and wide to the light-year
stars, lie back, and the sea will hold you.

EVENING

Evening: the fog rides in over small woods,
unrolling onto the garden made from the field.

In the house, the boy who planted the garden
takes his turn at putting together supper. The father,

who rented the house to have his time with the boy,
picks volunteer phlox by the edge of the woods.

The fog feels like rain, the garden needs sun. The boy
sets the table with spoons, then tosses three kinds

of lettuce, chopped scallions, spinach, and lots
of sliced cucumbers into a bowl. He passes his father

the ketchup. They sit on the two chipped chairs without
saying the blessing; the flowers the father put in a jar

grace the table. They have another week left.
Except for having to finish the postcard he's almost

written his mother, the boy is happy. Watching him
pour more ketchup onto his salad, his father

invents another new face. The boy grins.
His father points to the postcard; he washes up

by himself while the boy writes his mother.
Then his father reads the next chapter he promised.

The fog is all but asleep in the woods, evening
deepens the house; August has settled over the garden

the man and his son dug in June from the field.

JANE COOPER

Jane Cooper grew up in Jacksonville, Florida, and Princeton, New Jersey. We hear the gem-like music and currents of the St. John's River in her poems. Her father was one of the first practitioners of aviation law, and her uncle, Marion C. Cooper, was the creator of King Kong. She studied with Robert Lowell and John Berryman at the Iowa Writer's Workshop and has lived most of her life in New York City where she has been a teacher to several generations of poets. The title of Cooper's most recent collection, *Flashboat*, came to her in a dream. This title in many ways defines her work, a floating device, a source of security and survival; a boat that allows her to safely delve into lightning bright instances of the unknown and unexpected. She says that mystery and clarity have been her poetic concerns from the very beginning. Recently, Cooper has written a number of poems about aging, and about the desire to strip down to the most essential elements of life. "The Blue Anchor" is one of these poems; the lines have a sanded down quality to them as if she is sculpting light to reveal the soul. She says that as you get older you want to live with less baggage — in order to be open to other possibilities. The wonderful love poem "Rent" begins with a defensive gesture, but moves to a stance of confident vulnerability where love is defined not as a power play but as a "radiance of attention." The poem is both a challenge and a prayer.

THE BLUE ANCHOR

The future weighs down on me
just like a wall of light!

All these years
I've lived by necessity.
Now the world shines
like an empty room
clean all the way to the rafters.

The room might be waiting for its first tenants —
a bed, a chair, my old typewriter.

Or it might be Van Gogh's room
at Arles:
so neat, while his eyes grazed among phosphorus.
A blue anchor.

To live in the future
like a survivor!
Not the first step up the beach
but the second
then the third

— never forgetting
the wingprint of the mountain
over the fragile human settlement —

RENT

If you want my apartment, sleep in it
but let's have a clear understanding:
the books are still free agents.

If the rocking chair's arms surround you
they can also let you go,
they can shape the air like a body.

I don't want your rent, I want
a radiance of attention
like the candle's flame when we eat,

I mean a kind of awe
attending the spaces between us—
Not a roof but a field of stars.

ELIZABETH SPIRES

The birth of a child, the languid final days of summer—Elizabeth Spires is fascinated by life's beginnings and endings. Her voice is painterly and plainspoken. In her lines we encounter the land-locked Midwestern winters of her childhood, as well as the wide open afternoon views of the Atlantic Ocean. "On the Island" captures the light and rhythm of the sea, which Spires said she did not see until she was nineteen. The poem is a meditation on life cycles and aging, working against the stereotype that as we age we lose our power. "Easter Sunday 1955" is made more colorful by the fact that Spires never mentions a particular color in the poem; she allows us as readers to participate and fill in the scene with our own palette.

EASTER SUNDAY 1955

Why should anything go wrong in our bodies?
Why should we not be all beautiful?
Why should there be decay?—why death?
—and, oh, why, damnation?
            —Anthony Trollope, in a letter

What were we? What have we become?
Light fills the picture, the rising sun,
the three of us advancing, dreamlike,
up the steps of my grandparents' house on Oak Street.
Still young, my mother and father swing me
lightly up the steps, as if I weighed nothing.
From the shadows, my brother and sister watch,
wanting their turn, years away from being born.
Now my aunts and uncles and cousins
gather on the shaded porch of generation,
big enough for everyone. No one has died yet.
No vows have been broken. No words spoken
that can never be taken back, never forgotten.
I have a basket of eggs my mother and I dyed yesterday.
I ask my grandmother to choose one, just one,
and she takes me up—O hold me close!—
her cancer not yet diagnosed. I bury my face
in soft flesh, the soft folds of her Easter dress,
breathing her in, wanting to stay forever where I am.
Her death will be long and slow, she will beg
to be let go, and I will find myself, too quickly,
in the here-and-now moment of my fortieth year.
It's spring again. Easter. Now my daughter steps
into the light, her basket of eggs bright, so bright.
One, choose one, I hear her say, her face upturned

to mine, innocent of outcome. Beautiful child,
how thoughtlessly we enter the world!
How free we are, how bound, put here in love's name
—death's, too—to be happy if we can.

ON THE ISLAND
for Josephine Jacobsen

One ferry arrives as one is pulling out.
July was a high point, hot, bright and buttery.
August is huge and blue, a glittering gemstone
curving dangerously at either end into what precedes
and follows it. The ferry begins as a small white point
on the horizon and gradually enlarges into an event
we don't know whether to dread or impatiently wait for.
Those who have just disembarked look stunned and hopeful.
The trip has been long for them. Down the gangplank
they come, with dogs and bicycles and children,
the sun glaring down, the narrow streets of the town
crowded and loud. Weekends are always busiest.
Up the beach, we who have been here for weeks
are grateful to be going nowhere, to be innocent
bystanders to scenes of greeting and farewell.
We have lived through too many beginnings and ends,
and will again, but not today, thank goodness, not today.
Today we lean back lazily, our chairs set low in the sand,
happy to sit in the safe shadow of a big beach umbrella
and stare out at wide water, our minds emptying
like the plastic watering cans the children use
to wet down the sand. We coexist with them, dreaming
our dreams as they dream theirs, building our castles

in air, in sand, not minding when waves or wind
flood the moats and take down careful curling walls,
calmly rebuilding with the patience of clouds,
the dream we were dreaming beginning all over again.

But there is one among us who does not dream . . .
Waist-deep in rolling water, a woman, a grandmother,
stands in a skirted suit, a bright blue bathing cap
neatly fastened under her chin. Rock-solid, she strides
deeper into the cold blue water, calling back
to her two granddaughters, "Try to keep up with me, girls!"
Out beyond the breakers, she swims rapidly back and forth
between two unmarked points, then rests for a while,
her blue head buoyantly bobbing down and up.
Beaches are big enough for big thoughts that meander
like dogs, sniffing the truth out about themselves.
Will I, too, as I have secretly hoped, give myself up
one day to waves and water, no longer a watcher?
Will I lead the small ones out, fearlessly lead them out,
as if to say, "Courage, dear ones! Beauty will go. Pride, too.
We must take the plunge now or throw in the white towel!"

Like a huge bassoon, the inbound ferry sounds,
shaking the island. To leave here, all must ride it.
Some before others. Some at summer's end and some tomorrow.
Some never to return, and some to come back,
summer after summer, weaving a bright thread of constancy
into inconstant lives. Babies will change
into children, children will awkwardly grow up,
girls will find their slender beauty stolen,
and mothers will wake up grandmothers, they will wake up.
Pursued by change, they will run to the end of their lives,
no other choice left to them, and plunge into
an element darker than sunlight, darker than night.

The ever-widening wake of the inbound ferry
cannot shake the resolve of the woman in the waves.
She follows it out, waving her arms wildly
as she goes, not in distress, oh no,
but simply to give the ones going away a good goodbye.
Soon they will reach the mainland, the summer quickly
becoming a good dream to them, no turning point.
All will go on as it has. Or will it?
They point at the sight of a woman alone in a churning ocean
held up by . . . What holds her up? She waves and waves.
And they, not yet caught up in the life ahead of them,
wave back at her. They wave back.

ACKNOWLEDGMENTS

I wish to express my gratitude and appreciation to the poets gathered here and also to NPR's *All Things Considered* for featuring their work. I would especially like to acknowledge NPR producer extraordinaire Margaret Low Smith for her dedication in getting real poetry on the air and for making it all happen. Our collaboration from the very beginning was marked by a rare spontaneity, speed, openness, and freedom. It was a great pleasure working with her. I would also like to thank NPR's John Burnett, Jonathan Kern, Ellen Weiss, Noah Adams, and the wonderful Linda Wertheimer. Thanks to WFIU in Bloomington, also to Manoli Wetherell and Caryl Wheeler at the New York NPR Bureau. And thanks to the NPR affiliate radio stations around the country where we recorded the poems.

For early inspiration I am eternally grateful to Joseph Brodsky. My gratitude also to Bob Holman.

Many thanks to my agent the excellent Eileen Cope, and the tenacious Norman Kurz, contracts manager. Thanks also to my editor Diana Secker Larson. For support, advice, conversations, insights, and suggestions I would like to give multiple thanks and acknowledgment to Andy Biskin, Blythe Nobleman, Campbell McGrath, Janet Sorensen, Kevin Young, Stephanie Strickland, Melissa Stoeltjie, David Lehman, Walton Muyumba, Susan Lippman, Kirsten Nash, Eliza Griswold, Jessica Lewis Luck, Elizabeth Dodd, Gardner McFall, and Romayne Rubinas Dorsey. Thanks to my students and my teachers. Heartfelt thanks to my family, past and present. Many thanks also to Yaddo.

I am most grateful to the marvelous Sarah Wyatt who so graciously brought her acumen, kindness, and competence in helping me to edit, organize, type, and gather permissions for this manuscript.

Catherine Bowman was born in El Paso, Texas, and currently lives in Bloomington, Indiana, where she teaches at Indiana University. She has worked with NPR's *All Things Considered* since 1995 as a consultant and commentator on contemporary poetry. Her poems have appeared in *The Paris Review, Kenyon Review, TriQuarterly, The Best American Poetry,* and the *Los Angeles Times.* She is the award-winning author of two collections of poems, *1-800-HOT-RIBS* and *Rock Farm.*